The Guardian

QUICK CROSSWORDS 1

Published in 2021 by Welbeck
an imprint of Welbeck Non-Fiction,
part of Welbeck Publishing Group
20 Mortimer Street
London W1T 3JW

Text and Puzzles © 2021 Guardian News & Media Limited
Design © 2021 Welbeck Non-Fiction,
part of Welbeck Publishing Group

Editorial: Chris Mitchell
Design: Eliana Holder

A CIP catalogue for this book is available from the British
Library.

ISBN: 978-1-78739-694-4

Printed in the United Kingdom

10 9 8 7 6 5 4 3 2 1

The Guardian

QUICK CROSSWORDS 1

A collection of more than **200**
entertaining puzzles

WELBECK

About The Guardian

The Guardian has published honest and fearless journalism, free from commercial or political interference, since it was founded in 1821.

It now publishes a huge variety of puzzles every day, both online and in print, covering many different types of crosswords, sudoku, general knowledge quizzes and more.

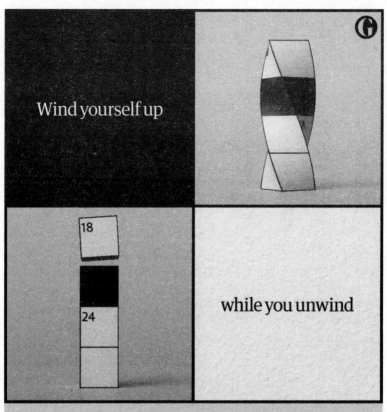

Introduction

Welcome to the first book in *The Guardian*'s brand-new puzzle series. The humble quick crossword puzzle has appeared in the pages of *The Guardian* for decades, and these crosswords have been curated especially from recent issues to form a bumper batch of pure enjoyment.

These crosswords are designed to be solvable in a short time – there are not mountains of clues to work through. However, they are not easy. While a crossword expert may be able to solve them in a single break in the day, it is much more likely that you will have to step away and return to them later. Try it – your mind has a pleasantly surprising way of working on the answers without you even knowing.

Above all, though, please enjoy this book! The world is full of challenges, but we hope that *these* challenges will provide a delightful diversion for you.

1

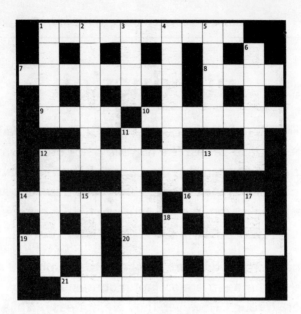

ACROSS

1 Soon (6,4)
7 Protesting vigorously (2,2,4)
8 Not at home (4)
9 Tax — obligation (4)
10 Unauthorised absence from school (7)
12 True tobacco (anag) — basis of chocolate (5,6)
14 Clergyman's gown (7)
16 Wealthy (4)
19 Adhesive (4)
20 Become pregnant (8)
21 Contrite (10)

DOWN

1 Creature with two feet (5)
2 Zealot (7)
3 Uncommon (4)
4 Glossy (8)
5 Large African antelope (5)
6 Part of a tea set (6)
11 Ludicrous (8)
12 Hold gently and protectively (6)
13 Cut into three parts (7)
15 Slumber (5)
17 Mayhem (5)
18 Drawback (4)

Solution see page 233

2

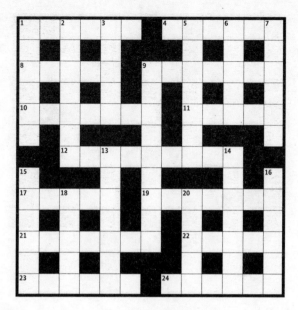

ACROSS

1 Kind of watch chain (6)
4 Annoy persistently (6)
8 US world heavyweight boxing champion, b.1966 — English fast bowler, d. 2015 (5)
9 Passed out (7)
10 Oxford academic notable for mixing up his syllables when talking, d. 1930 (7)
11 English poet, said to be 'mad, bad, and dangerous to know', d. 1824 (5)
12 Working in a well-organised and competent way (9)
17 Piggy noises (5)
19 Enthusiastic and loud applause (sometimes standing) (7)
21 Home providing care for the sick (7)
22 Lowest male singing voice (sometimes 'profundo') (5)
23 Stella (anag) — waiting to go (3,3)
24 Petition to a deity (6)

DOWN

1 Condition involving impaired social interaction (6)
2 Made to order (7)
3 Quarrel (3-2)
5 Of a sweet and friendly disposition (7)
6 Lustful woodland god — stray (anag) (5)
7 Finale (6)
9 Take back property because mortgage payments due have not been paid (9)
13 Offering fun and gaiety (7)
14 Parched (7)
15 Moses's successor, victor of the Battle of Jericho (6)
16 Taking place within a building (6)
18 Through the nose? (5)
20 Medium to dark brownish-yellow colour (5)

Solution see page 233

3

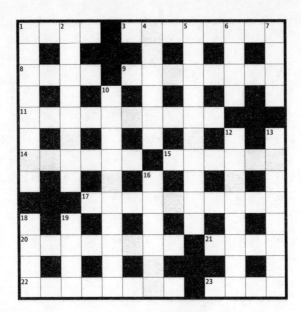

ACROSS

1 Covering for the wrist (4)
3 Likened (8)
8 Relocate (4)
9 Non-military (8)
11 Fiendish (10)
14 Riches (6)
15 Middle (6)
17 Genealogical chart (6,4)
20 Improved (8)
21 Person regularly 'economical with the truth' (4)
22 Left over (8)
23 Regard lecherously (4)

DOWN

1 Loss of status (8)
2 Recommended consumption of fruit and veg (4,1,3)
4 Egyptian god, father of Horus (6)
5 Detective (7,3)
6 Incursion (4)
7 Unpleasantly wet and cold (4)
10 Smuggled goods (10)
12 Dying of hunger (8)
13 Practise (8)
16 Filmdom (6)
18 Prickly adhesive seed case (4)
19 A long, long time (4)

Solution see page 233

4

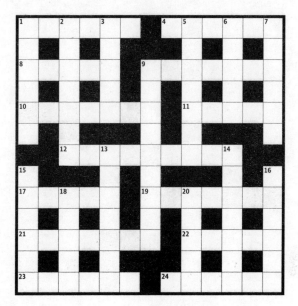

ACROSS

1 Accepted practice (6)
4 Type of shellfish (6)
8 Particular environment (5)
9 Matrimony (7)
10 Fraught with danger (7)
11 Drive back (5)
12 Daring (9)
17 Fire-raising (5)
19 Provide physical or mental relief — satisfy (7)
21 Heckle (7)
22 Warble (5)
23 Second version of film (6)
24 Deliberately stay clear of (6)

DOWN

1 (Of the sea) a bit rough (6)
2 Region to which Russian and then Soviet governments sent those considered disloyal (7)
3 Surpass (5)
5 Cook too briefly (7)
6 Tread angrily (5)
7 Probable (6)
9 Ironic and/or witty quip (9)
13 Monarchy, a member of the European Union (7)
14 Abjectly subservient (7)
15 Hair trimmer (6)
16 Custard-coloured (6)
18 Play badly on a guitar (5)
20 Locations (5)

Solution see page 233

5

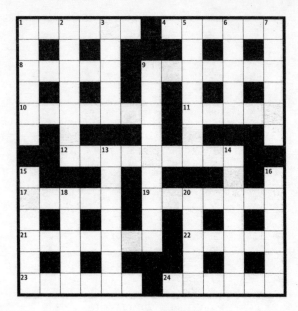

ACROSS

1 Rest (6)
4 Academy awards (6)
8 Band of people involved in some activity (5)
9 Card game (7)
10 Timorous (7)
11 Unconcealed (5)
12 Assessment (9)
17 Arms and legs (5)
19 Mercury alloy (7)
21 Charming (7)
22 Consciousness of one's wrongdoing (5)
23 Cease (6)
24 Dazed (6)

DOWN

1 Swindle (3-3)
2 Sieved tomato purée (7)
3 Projecting underwater ridge (5)
5 Wavy — winding (7)
6 Domicile (5)
7 Soundness of mind (6)
9 Grimace (4,1,4)
13 Handguns (7)
14 Insulation — failing to keep up (7)
15 Scratched (6)
16 Mildly obscene (6)
18 Less (5)
20 Soothsayer (5)

Solution see page 234

6

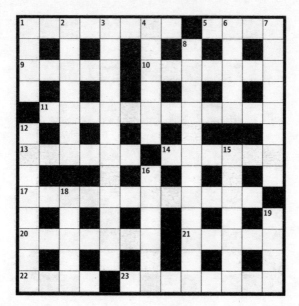

ACROSS

1 Socially pretentious woman (4,4)
5 Party — clobber (4)
9 Thrash about (5)
10 Lustful (7)
11 Unfair (5,3,4)
13 Major blood vessel (6)
14 Doctor-priest working with magic (6)
17 Surfaced area for parking vehicles (12)
20 Most tidy (7)
21 Brideshead Revisited author, d. 1966 (5)
22 Adam and Eve's third son (4)
23 One who's owed money (8)

DOWN

1 Vitality (4)
2 Vernacular (7)
3 Starved (12)
4 Morally pure (6)
6 Love deeply (5)
7 Indecisive (8)
8 Presaged (12)
12 Great quantity (8)
15 Organised search for a fugitive (7)
16 Synagogue official who conducts the liturgical part of the service (6)
18 Reprimand — cook (5)
19 Make a humming noise (4)

Solution see page 234

7

ACROSS

5 Sanctified (11)
7 Make tea (or beer) (4)
8 In good spirits (8)
9 Cautionary advice (7)
11 Paunch (5)
13 Code for I (5)
14 Church cushion (7)
16 Waterfall — eye complaint (8)
17 Needy (4)
18 Deep cuts or tears in the flesh (11)

DOWN

1 Bite persistently (4)
2 Ancestry — downward movement (7)
3 Set of containers for salt, pepper, oil, vinegar etc (5)
4 Naked (8)
5 Appearance of performers on stage to acknowledge applause (7,4)
6 Swindle (6-5)
10 Pain in the neck (8)
12 Musical setting of a text (7)
15 Raced (anag) — small inner group of activists (5)
17 Story line (4)

Solution see page 234

8

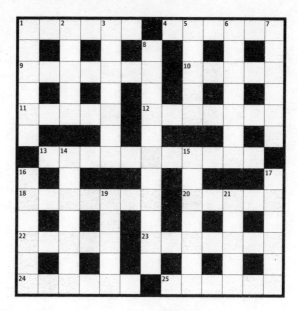

ACROSS

1 Overcast (6)
4 German dramatist and poet who wrote The Threepenny Opera, d.1956 (6)
9 Knock down (3,4)
10 Climbing plant of the pea family, cultivated as fodder (5)
11 Fault (5)
12 Dashing and debonair young man (7)
13 Regular failure to turn up for work (11)
18 Ceremonially impure (7)
20 Tree of the birch family (5)
22 Immature form of an insect before metamorphosis (5)
23 Flammable liquid hydrocarbon mixture (7)
24 Highly motivated (6)
25 Committed to memory (6)

DOWN

1 Large wader of the sandpiper family (6)
2 Possessor (5)
3 Varied (7)
5 Bolero composer, d. 1937 (5)
6 Short curved naval sword (7)
7 South Pacific island where both Robert Louis Stevenson and Paul Gauguin spent time (6)
8 Causing alarm (11)
14 White rum, first produced in Cuba (7)
15 Specimen (7)
16 Greek mathematician, d. mid-3rd century BC (6)
17 Out-and-out (6)
19 Fill with high spirits (5)
21 Discourage (5)

Solution see page 234

9

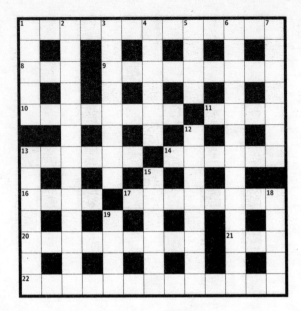

ACROSS

5 Henry Ford's view of the past (more or less) (7,2,4)
8 Friend (3)
9 Toe and heel clicking performer (3,6)
10 Hackneyed (8)
11 Reptile (abbr) (4)
13 Hooray! (6)
14 Norway lobsters — Dublin Bay prawns (6)
16 Persian emperor (4)
17 Pay (8)
20 Emeer's duo (anag) — tiny hornless ruminant (5,4)
21 Head-swivelling bird (3)
22 Distant but familiar relative (7,6)

DOWN

1 Large wallower (abbr) (5)
2 Pub nibbles (6,7)
3 Butted in (8)
4 Prepay (anag) — an excited puppy? (6)
5 Junk messages (4)
6 Informal (13)
7 Pakistan's most populous city (7)
12 Outline — setting for a novel (8)
13 Muslim women's veil (7)
15 Rotten rotter (3,3)
18 Hairdressing establishment (5)
19 Abominable snowman (4)

Solution see page 235

10

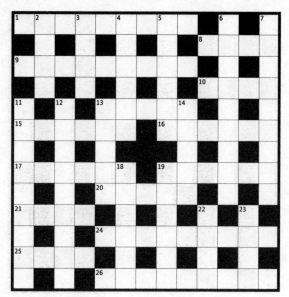

ACROSS

1 Quip (9)

8 Sow's mate (4)

9 Silly person (with sparrow's mind?) (9)

10 Procreated (4)

13 Racist or sexist? (5)

15 Rescue (anag) (6)

16 Shellfish soup (6)

17 Strain (6)

19 Spanish wine shop (6)

20 Refuse with contempt (5)

21 Give out (4)

24 Priceless! (9)

25 Sea eagle (4)

26 Desire to travel (5,4)

DOWN

2 Wading bird (4)

3 Rise and fall of the sea (4)

4 Knitted jacket that buttons up the front (abbr) (6)

5 Bicycle-like device for sliding down snow slopes (3-3)

6 Nickname – Boers quit (anag) (9)

7 Path for horses (9)

11 Kind of triangle (9)

12 Arachnids with a sting in the tail (9)

13 Copper and zinc alloy (5)

14 Big hybrid of the cat family (5)

18 Run fast (6)

19 Bring up for discussion (6)

22 Lovers' row (4)

23 Fibre used for making sacking and ropes (4)

Solution see page 235

11

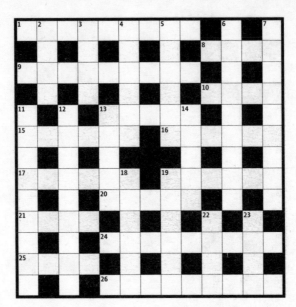

ACROSS

1 Refraining from alcohol (9)

8 With a feeling of comfort and warmth (4)

9 Study of the supposed influence of stars and planets on our affairs (9)

10 One divines the future (4)

13 Show cynical contempt (5)

15 Spies (6)

16 Jacket worn by a herald (6)

17 Win a victory over (6)

19 Pivots about which levers turn (6)

20 Confusion (3–2)

21 Nobleman (4)

24 Poor physical condition (3,6)

25 Luxurious hotel (4)

26 Famous (9)

DOWN

2 Outback (4)

3 Expression (4)

4 Sheer stockings (6)

5 Lump of valuable metal (6)

6 Marriage based on real affection (4,5)

7 Vehicle with two different propulsion systems (6,3)

11 Hispanic outlaw — or old bean (anag) (9)

12 Make holes in (9)

13 Very hot water? (5)

14 Sewed together quickly (3,2)

18 Handle of a rudder (6)

19 South-west London football club (6)

22 Hock (4)

23 Flabbergast (4)

Solution see page 235

12

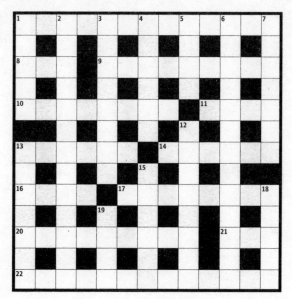

ACROSS

1 Hanging item to protect a theatre audience (6,7)
8 Botham or Chappell? (3)
9 Government treasury department (9)
10 Hand-held firework (8)
11 Unit of heredity (4)
13 Sesame-seed based foodstuff (6)
14 Viz (6)
16 Style (4)
17 Furtive (8)
20 Mysterious items — ciao trees (anag) (9)
21 Point (3)
22 Tease (4,3,6)

DOWN

1 From Zurich, say? (5)
2 Type of cured fish (6,7)
3 Arduous walking (8)
4 Distinction (6)
5 Stink (4)
6 Funfair (9,4)
7 Where young plants grow up? (7)
12 Atomic bomb target, 9 August 1945 (8)
13 Violent disturbance (7)
15 Discord (6)
18 That tastes great! (5)
19 Infernal nuisance (4)

Solution see page 235

13

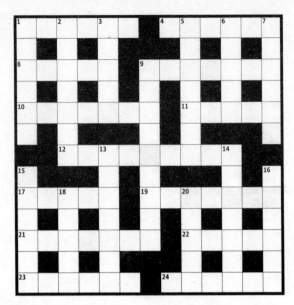

ACROSS

1 Relaxed (6)
4 Rejects with contempt (6)
8 Exhibition of cowboy skills (5)
9 Person who shoes horses (7)
10 Non-religious (7)
11 Artist's supporting frame (5)
12 Pharmacist (9)
17 In town (or city) (5)
19 Haute couture (7)
21 Wicked (7)
22 Identifying name (5)
23 Gloomy (6)
24 Motor fuel (6)

DOWN

1 Fondle (6)
2 Lured — enticed (7)
3 Coral island surrounding a lagoon (5)
5 Port of Athens (7)
6 Searches by police without warning (5)
7 Walk in a leisurely way (6)
9 Distracted (9)
13 Spanish drink of red wine with soda or lemonade (7)
14 Engage in noisy merrymaking (7)
15 Interred (6)
16 Temper by heat treatment (6)
18 Bulges (5)
20 French composer of the Gymnopédies, d. 1925 (5)

Solution see page 236

14

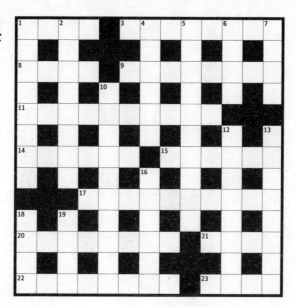

ACROSS

1 Attitude (4)
3 Activate (6,2)
8 Rake (4)
9 Tactful type (8)
11 Excessive eater (6,4)
14 Boulevard (6)
15 Trash (6)
17 Indicator that goes right round hourly (6,4)
20 Type of retriever (8)
21 Compact (4)
22 Surrounded by enemies (8)
23 Semi-precious stone used in making cameos (4)

DOWN

1 Landlocked South American country (8)
2 Implement used by windowcleaners (8)
4 Grumble (6)
5 Discuss a matter straightforwardly (4,6)
6 Pot plant (4)
7 Do, re or mi? (4)
10 Judge (10)
12 Unwelcome intrusion (8)
13 Form of concrete (5-3)
16 To-do (6)
18 Thick flat piece of stone (4)
19 Bird sacred in Ancient Egypt (4)

Solution see page 236

15

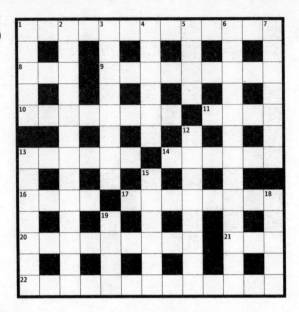

ACROSS

1 Win a race (6,3,4)
8 Pull (3)
9 Concerning (2,7)
10 Don't mention it! (3,2,3)
11 Make well (4)
13 Used the horn (6)
14 Deny any connection with (6)
16 Time period (4)
17 Refusing to come to terms with a painful reality (2,6)
20 Useful facilities (9)
21 Enjoyment (3)
22 In good shape (4,3,6)

DOWN

1 Conductor's wand (5)
2 Scottish dance (9,4)
3 Skimpy knickers (8)
4 Excitement (6)
5 Ova (4)
6 Stop trying to persuade someone that you are right and they are wrong (5,2,6)
7 Greek letter (7)
12 Movie buff — tie canes (anag) (8
13 Track beside a canal (7)
15 Relax (6)
18 Gangling (5)
19 Kind of bean (4))

Solution see page 236

16

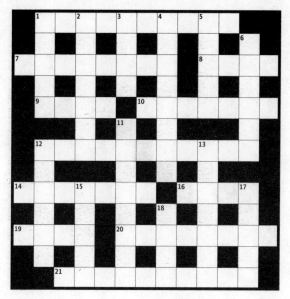

ACROSS

1 Fortress (10)
7 Briefly and clearly expressed (8)
8 Hard by (4)
9 Sulky expression (4)
10 Dignity (anag) (7)
12 One employed to look after a golf course (11)
14 Grapple (7)
16 Two-masted square-rigged sailing ship (4)
19 Unreliable old car (4)
20 Drying-up cloth (3,5)
21 Ornamental stand for plants (10)

DOWN

1 Baffle (5)
2 Hermit (7)
3 Grandma (4)
4 Direct telephone links for use in an emergency (8)
5 Island in the Bristol Channel (5)
6 Leather worker — old coin (6)
11 Blown up (8)
12 Precious stone, usually red (6)
13 Intention (7)
15 Reddish-brown (5)
17 Long-necked, migratory aquatic birds (5)
18 Farm outbuilding (4)

Solution see page 236

17

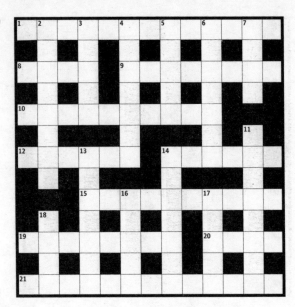

ACROSS

1 In the main (13)
8 Quick and agile (4)
9 Scaremonger (8)
10 Bewilders (10)
12 Wheel and deal (6)
14 Wound (6)
15 Allure (10)
19 Arithmetic operation (8)
20 Osculate (4)
21 Alone and unaided (13)

DOWN

2 Censure (8)
3 Forget one's lines (3,2)
4 Quantify (7)
5 Approaches (5)
6 Retribution (7)
7 Missing (4)
11 Gigantic (8)
13 Deliberately vague (7)
14 Well-read (7)
16 Race (5)
17 Kidnapped (5)
18 Industrial oven (4)

Solution see page 237

18

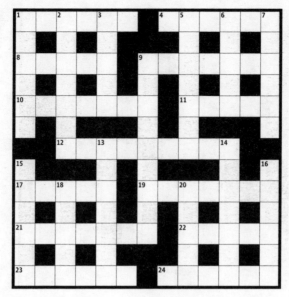

ACROSS

1 Appease (6)
4 Court game (6)
8 Ardent male lover (5)
9 Human corpse (7)
10 Having a soft spot for (5,2)
11 Eurasian primrose with yellow flowers (5)
12 Turned aside (9)
17 Fish eater of the weasel family (5)
19 Brother or sister (7)
21 Sweet sauce of eggs and milk (7)
22 Coffee served with hot milk (5)
23 Vent (6)
24 Of mixed ancestry (6)

DOWN

1 Go off (6)
2 Praise formally (7)
3 Defy (orders etc) (5)
5 Last in the line (7)
6 Where the umbilical cord was once attached (5)
7 Screenplay (6)
9 Abridged (9)
13 Run cafe (anag) — very hot place (7)
14 Itinerant (7)
15 South American cloak (6)
16 Settled by common consent (6)
18 Goggle–box (2,3)
20 Large and unwieldy (5)

Solution see page 237

19

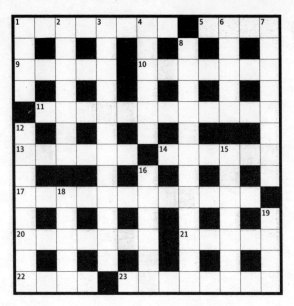

ACROSS

1 Pyrotechnic device (8)
5 Called (4)
9 Thigh bone (5)
10 Easily bent (7)
11 Wind snatcher (anag) — fork-tailed bird (8,4)
13 Set of clothing (6)
14 Wood (6)
17 Device used for breaking down doors (9,3)
20 Novelty (7)
21 Invert (5)
22 Challenge (4)
23 Marauding creature (8)

DOWN

1 Historic Scottish county (and kingdom) (4)
2 Surviving fragment (7)
3 Tim Berners-Lee's invention (5,4,3)
4 Go — mend (6)
6 Move at an easy pace (5)
7 Verdure (8)
8 Money raised to finance a campaign (8,4)
12 Joined (8)
15 Most valiant (7)
16 Mouth (slang) (6)
18 Tall building (5)
19 River that, with the Neisse, forms the German-Polish border (4)

Solution see page 237

20

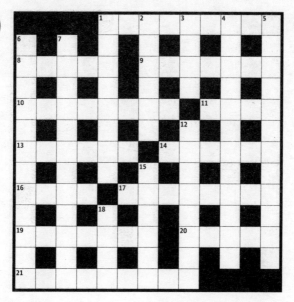

ACROSS

1 Bottle opener (9)
8 Adult insect post-metamorphosis (5)
9 Warlike (7)
10 Incidentally (2,3,3)
11 Group of players (4)
13 Eraser (6)
14 Heavy non-venomous snake (6)
16 Auditory organs (4)
17 Counters (anag) — interpret (8)
19 Made possible (7)
20 Small wood (5)
21 Lasting a very short time (9)

DOWN

1 Confined to a small space (8)
2 __ MacDonald, first British Labour PM (6)
3 Certain (4)
4 Make a lot of noise (5,3,4)
5 Polite (4-8)
6 Payment of money from a fund (12)
7 Coastal resort city in southern California (5,7)
12 Vision (8)
15 Easy task (6)
18 In addition (4)

Solution see page 237

21

ACROSS

1 Self-governing American commonwealth in the Caribbean (6,4)

7 Person bringing charges (7)

8 Bout (5)

10 The Garden of England (4)

11 American thriller or detective movie style of the '40s and '50s (4,4)

13 Drink of the gods (6)

15 11am meal? (6)

17 Defamed (8)

18 You in olden times (4)

21 Cheeky (5)

22 President of Egypt, 1981–2011 (7)

23 In a position to reach a goal without much further difficulty (4,3,3)

DOWN

1 Nut tree of the southern United States and Mexico (5)

2 Direction taken when going from the US towards Ireland (4)

3 Pompous and boring (6)

4 Herb with narrow leaves (8)

5 Witty drawing (7)

6 Mule, for example (4,6)

9 Strong tremor (10)

12 Spout ending in a grotesquely carved figure (8)

14 Improvised song of the Caribbean (7)

16 Address of a religious nature (6)

19 Annoy continually (5)

20 Retired (4)

Solution see page 238

22

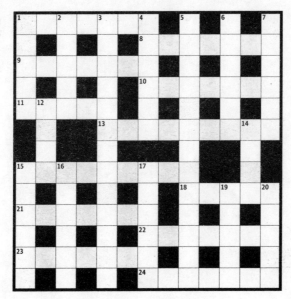

ACROSS

1 Actor's assistant (7)
8 Set apart (7)
9 Of the heart (7)
10 Having written a valid will (7)
11 TS Eliot's 'cruelest month' (5)
13 Irascibility (9)
15 Someone who changes position to suit the situation (9)
18 Contemptible person (5)
21 Debauchee (7)
22 Rollicking (7)
23 Cost (7)
24 American–born British sculptor, d. 1959 (7)

DOWN

1 Russian country house (5)
2 Trial and ___ (5)
3 Give away secrets (5,3,5)
4 Rustic (anag) — gaping grimace (6)
5 Scrupulous (13)
6 Glass flask for serving wine (6)
7 Break for holiday (6)
12 Established route (4)
14 Cause trouble (4)
15 Police officer (slang) (6)
16 Unexpected — precipitous (6)
17 Freedom of access (6)
19 Wear away (5)
20 Largest port in South Korea (5)

Solution see page 238

23

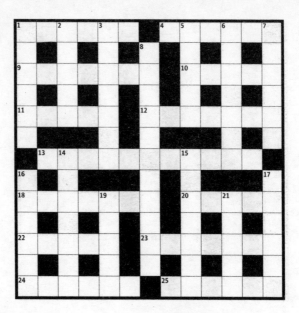

ACROSS

1 One who's hooked (6)
4 Young cattle (6)
9 Sugar present in milk (7)
10 Racing pigeon? (5)
11 Theme park features (5)
12 Satan (3,4)
13 Downcast (11)
18 Entrenched stronghold (7)
20 Welsh dog (5)
22 Annual grass with light brown grains (5)
23 Renounced (7)
24 Hurried (6)
25 AM/PM separator? (6)

DOWN

1 Attraction (6)
2 Played with small cubes (5)
3 Rich old king (7)
5 Felt pain (5)
6 Bloodsucker (7)
7 Butcher-bird (6)
8 Give vent to anger (3,3,5)
14 Compensation (7)
15 Tetanus (7))
16 Box-like container that slides (6)
17 Centre (6)
19 Loosen (5)
21 Connected with farming (5)

Solution see page 238

24

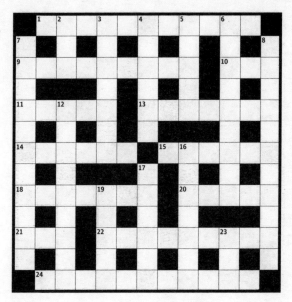

ACROSS

1 Consisting of small disconnected parts (11)
9 Annexe (9)
10 Sheep (3)
11 Shocking weapon (5)
13 Animal — per load (anag) (7)
14 Imitates satirically (6)
15 Lurid (6)
18 Give a spoken account (7)
20 Well-groomed (5)
21 Perform(ance) (3)
22 Invoke evil — crime tape (anag) (9)
24 Needless (11)

DOWN

2 Furrow caused by wheels (3)
3 Applicable to an entire class (7)
4 Fit to eat (6)
5 Ballroom dance (for two?) (5)
6 Look into again (2-7)
7 Reference (11)
8 Submit (4,3,4)
12 Good person who helps another in distress (9)
16 Solutions (7)
17 Highly emotional film (6)
19 Tolerate (5)
23 Atmosphere (of a melody?) (3)

Solution see page 238

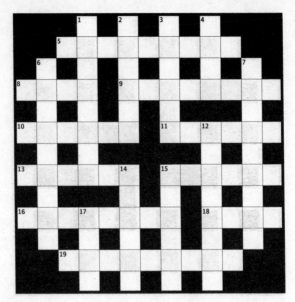

ACROSS

5 Resist (9)
8 Soon (4)
9 Testimony — verification (8)
10 UK shipping forecast area (6)
11 Shady garden alcove (6)
13 Cause to be loved (6)
15 Cry — snitch (6)
16 Unwelcome visitor (8)
18 Food (for a friar?) (4)
19 Savagely fierce (9)

DOWN

1 Highest point (8)
2 Joyful — optimistic (6)
3 King of the Huns, d. 453 (6)
4 Leg joint (4)
6 Angered by unjust treatment (9)
7 Residence (9)
12 Utter impulsively (5,3)
14 Very exciting — glowing (3-3)
15 Morally degraded (6)
17 South American flightless bird (4)

Solution see page 239

26

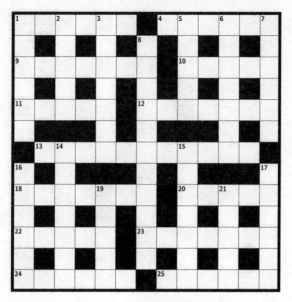

ACROSS

1 Look out (6)
4 Given a sweetener (6)
9 Keenly excited (7)
10 Chores (5)
11 Device producing an intense beam of light (5)
12 Had nice (anag) — spiny anteater (7)
13 Attract a great deal of attention (4,1,6)
18 Pilot (7)
20 Creator of Eeyore (5)
22 Spanish red wine (5)
23 Chilean desert (7)
24 Much obliged (6)
25 Stir up (6)

DOWN

1 Small hound (6)
2 Collection of closely packed trees (5)
3 Book — store (7)
5 Strain, as if to vomit (5)
6 As well as (7)
7 Deprive of the rights of a barrister (6)
8 Combative (11)
14 The Grand Canyon State (7)
15 Lower back ache (7)
16 Attic (6)
17 21 (6)
19 Pursue (5)
21 Time off (5)

Solution see page 239

27

ACROSS

1 Marvel (6)
4 Pastimes (5)
7 Arousing sexual desire (6)
8 Small pointed beard (6)
9 Afrikaans speaker (4)
10 Out of the way (8)
12 Africa's highest mountain (11)
17 Dry brandy from south-west France (8)
19 Ooze (4)
20 Court sport (6)
21 Permanent polar cover (3,3)
22 Summary of articles of religious belief (5)
23 Give sworn evidence (6)

DOWN

1 Male witch (7)
2 Without affectation (7)
3 Old smuggler's foe (9)
4 Menacing animal sound (5)
5 Bullfighter (7)
6 Rapid (6)
11 Draftee (9)
13 Huge (7)
14 Severely simple (7)
15 Ham it up (7)
16 European sea (6)
18 Medieval association of merchants (5)

Solution see page 239

28

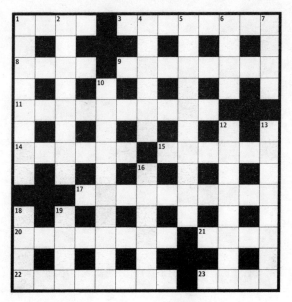

ACROSS

1 Release a long breath (4)
3 Impeccable (8)
8 Excessively forward (4)
9 Evocative (8)
11 Instrument measuring speed of rotation (10)
14 Squalid (6)
15 Skit (6)
17 Poster-securing device? (7,3)
20 Area furthest from the stumps (8)
21 Old South American (4)
22 Old film about current events (8)
23 Tiny piece (4)

DOWN

1 Wreck (8)
2 Wedge from Royal Portrush? (4,4)
4 Grey and overcast (6)
5 Child prodigy (10)
6 Way to go! (4)
7 Powdery starch used in cooking (4)
10 Royal Artillery soldier (10)
12 Get a move on! (4,2,2)
13 Ghostly figure — man's path (anag) (8)
16 Three fours (6)
18 Urban area (4)
19 Keep (4)

Solution see page 239

29

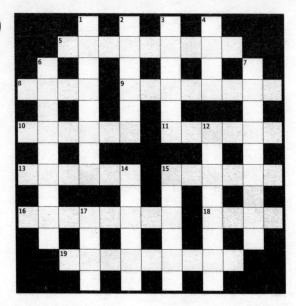

ACROSS

5 Score of three strokes under par for a golf hole (9)

8 Stare stupidly (4)

9 Pierce with a sharp point (8)

10 Mischievous child (6)

11 Be waiting for (6)

13 Largest New World vulture (6)

15 Thin — inadequate (6)

16 Derived support from (6,2)

18 Submissive (4)

19 Maybe (9)

DOWN

1 Carelessly executed (8)

2 Speed up (6)

3 Polished — sophisticated (6)

4 Applications (4)

6 Car with a folding top — trace boil (anag) (9)

7 Identified by close investigation (9)

12 Dispensary (8)

14 Censor part of a text for security reasons (6)

15 Involving human effort (6)

17 Require(ment) (4)

Solution see page 240

30

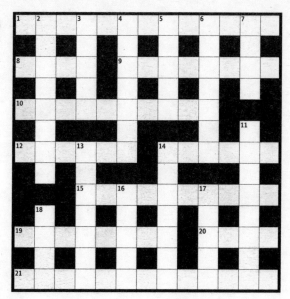

ACROSS

1 Anthracite or charcoal, for example — foul elk messes (anag) (9,4)

8 Some time back (4)

9 Female server (8)

10 Well, well! (8,2)

12 Toothed fastener (6)

14 Sour-tasting leaves used in salads and sauces (6)

15 Censure (10)

19 Northernmost of the Windward Islands (8)

20 Cloistered brother (4)

21 State of extreme joy (7,6)

DOWN

2 Small guitar-like instrument (8)

3 Work dough (5)

4 It's engaged while driving up or down a steep hill (3,4)

5 Helvetic (5)

6 Person who writes comedies — fur care (anag) (7)

7 Orient (4)

11 Succession of ordered things (8)

13 Side view (7)

14 Tummy (7)

16 Dot — full stop (5)

17 Afro-Cuban dance (5)

18 Counterspy (4)

Solution see page 240

31

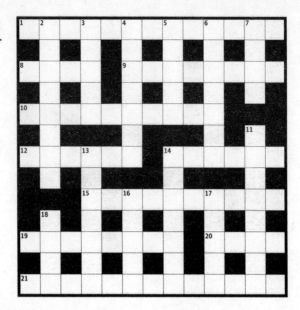

ACROSS

1 Children's party game (7,6)
8 Thin coating (4)
9 West (8)
10 Period of enforced isolation (10)
12 Unintelligent (6)
14 Methodical procedure (6)
15 Shame claim (anag) — 29 September (10)
19 Left high and dry (8)
20 Grown-up kid (4)
21 Children's party game (4,3,6)

DOWN

2 Omnipresence (8)
3 Turkish seaport, formerly called Smyrna (5)
4 Embellished (7)
5 Spiny desert plants (5)
6 Formal speech (7)
7 Status — row (4)
11 Standing apart (8)
13 Self-important (7)
14 Comedian (5-2)
16 Large shell (5)
17 Light beer (5)
18 Festive occasion — variety of apple (4)

Solution see page 240

32

ACROSS

1 Summarised — lacking concentration (10)

7 Blew one's own trumpet (7)

8 Famous (5)

10 Widely held misconception (4)

11 Statement of a company's financial affairs (8)

13 Firmly attached — arrested (6)

15 Cheap and vulgar behaviour (6)

17 Dance hall (8)

18 Made very cold (4)

21 Identified as the best (5)

22 Leave behind (7)

23 Good health! (3,3,4)

DOWN

1 Expect (5)

2 Wise — herb (4)

3 Lessen (6)

4 Kiss and cuddle (8)

5 Country on the Baltic (7)

6 Causing moral revulsion (10)

9 Progeny (10)

12 Most intoxicated? (8)

14 Animosity (3,4)

16 Contribute charitably (6)

19 Military trainee (5)

20 Garment — promontory (4)

Solution see page 240

33

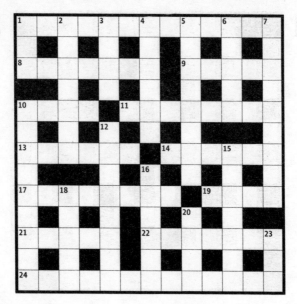

ACROSS

1 Person experienced in life (3,2,3,5)

8 Vandal (7)

9 Comes closer to (5)

10 Team up (with) (4)

11 Day of very hot and sunny weather (8)

13 Completely saturated (6)

14 Wood cut and prepared as building material (6)

17 Discursive (8)

19 Badly behaved child (4)

21 Machine that produces the winning Premium Bond numbers (5)

22 Blood disorder — ie I am Ana (anag) (7)

24 Get married? (4,3,6)

DOWN

1 Cut the grass (3)

2 Irritated (7)

3 Bogus (4)

4 Roman lyric poet, d.8BC — a chore (anag) (6)

5 Inspiring a feeling of delight (8)

6 Limits within which something can be effective (5)

7 Member of the British 7th Armoured Division in North Africa, 1941-2 (6,3)

10 Able to soak up liquid easily (9)

12 Determined to achieve something at all costs (4-4)

15 Female star of the 1942 film Casablanca, d.1982 (7)

16 Provoke to fury (6)

18 Capital of Belarus (5)

20 Welcome — precipitation (4)

23 Chopper (3)

Solution see page 241

34

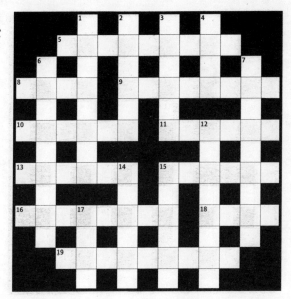

ACROSS

5 Cavalier's foe (9)

8 Abel's brother (4)

9 Predicament (8)

10 Scam — musical instrument (6)

11 Further up (6)

13 Gratitude (6)

15 Don Quixote's squire, ___ Panza (6)

16 Where light meals may be bought (5,3)

18 Sneering look (4)

19 Elongated (9)

DOWN

1 Took part (6,2)

2 Unlike anything else (6)

3 Beat soundly (6)

4 Stiff paper (4)

6 Disappearing (9)

7 Priceless newspaper (9)

12 Taller and thinner (8)

14 Curved cavalry swords (6)

15 Allowing no deviation (6)

17 Appealing — cunning (4)

Solution see page 241

35

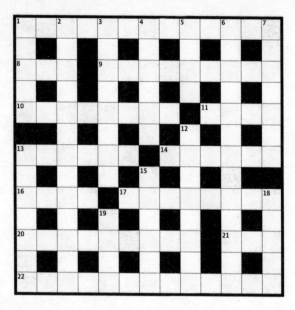

ACROSS

1 Corporate raider who sells off parts of a company for personal gain (5,8)

8 Indian state, former Portuguese colony (3)

9 Boring hard cheese (informal) (9)

10 Quickness (8)

11 Form of hydrated silica, often used as a gemstone (4)

13 Clergyman (6)

14 Exist permanently as part of (6)

16 Contest of speed (4)

17 Kept within limits (8)

20 Small thin sausage (9)

21 Be prostrate (3)

22 Someone excessively affected by a hard luck story (8,5)

DOWN

1 Rage (5)

2 Unscrupulous dealing (5,8)

3 Shyness (8)

4 Provokes — a stunt (anag) (6)

5 Two people considered together (informal) (4)

6 Odds and ends used in a particular pursuit (13)

7 Beat back (7)

12 Instantly (2,1,5)

13 Woody centre of an ear of maize (7)

15 Region (6)

18 Inhabited (5)

19 River crossing (4)

Solution see page 241

36

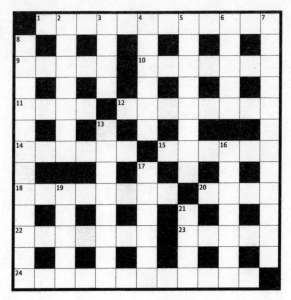

ACROSS

1 Understood (12)

9 Musical composition with a theme repeated and developed (5)

10 Gun (7)

11 One of the Great Lakes (4)

12 European capital (8)

14 Unexpected and inexplicable change (6)

15 Commonly repeated word or phrase (6)

18 Marine mollusc (3,5)

20 Rebuff (4)

22 Bar — omit (7)

23 Freight (5)

24 Idle chatter (6–6)

DOWN

2 Currently in progress (7)

3 Writer of verse (4)

4 Strenuous exertion (6)

5 Centaurs (anag) — native of an ancient state of central Italy (8)

6 Cover loosely with a cloth (5)

7 11th-century land survey of England (8,4)

8 Fizzy (12)

13 Serene (8)

16 Clinging part of a plant (7)

17 Credit (anag) — steer (6)

19 Racecourse, home to the Gold Cup since 1807 (5)

21 Deer's tail (4)

Solution see page 241

37

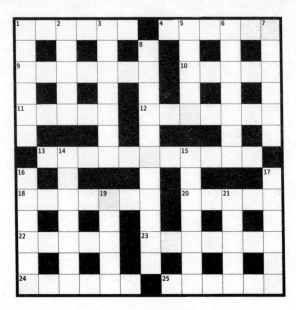

ACROSS

1 Eat greedily (like a turkey?) (6)
4 Backhanders (6)
9 Endeavour (7)
10 Interior layout and furnishings (5)
11 Dull persistent pains (5)
12 Capital of Madeira (7)
13 Everyday (11)
18 Poison, As (7)
20 Deep ravine (5)
22 Shout of approval (5)
23 Hug (7)
24 Endured (6)
25 Closely joined (6)

DOWN

1 Leave (2,4)
2 Markedly masculine (5)
3 Amount of money paid all at once (4,3)
5 Sculptor of The Thinker (5)
6 Relating to the Greek god of wine (7)
7 High-pitched and piercing (6)
8 Arrogantly obstinate (5-6)
14 Edible bivalve molluscs (7)
15 Able to be read (7)
16 17th century French mathematician — SI unit of pressure (6)
17 Saw (6)
19 Scandinavian (5)
21 Dahl or Amundsen? (5)

Solution see page 242

38

ACROSS

1 Refute (10)

7 Spiked attachment for a climbing boot (7)

8 Council of the clergy (5)

10 Putrid (4)

11 Negligent (8)

13 Fire-breathing monster (6)

15 Cover for holding loose papers together (6)

17 Aesthetically pleasing (8)

18 Tiresome person — tidal flood (4)

21 Obtuse — impenetrable (5)

22 Tool with hooks for grasping and holding (7)

23 Caught by surprise — I did blends (anag) (10)

DOWN

1 22 yards (5)

2 Back of the neck (4)

3 Learnt (anag) — lease (6)

4 Word blindness (8)

5 Maintain (7)

6 Certified officially (10)

9 Unruly (10)

12 Expected (8)

14 Weapons store (7)

16 Old Testament book (6)

19 Had — endow (anag) (5)

20 Unyielding (4)

Solution see page 242

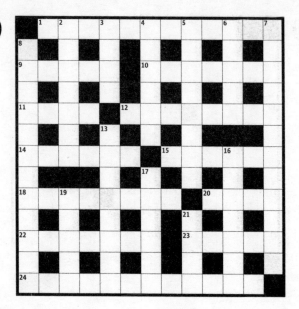

ACROSS

1 In the intervals separating other activities (7,5)

9 Scope (5)

10 Confusion (7)

11 Small island in a river (4)

12 Impoverished — ending it (anag) (8)

14 Protective headgear (6)

15 Grapes (anag) — cigarette (slang) (6)

18 Much employed (4,4)

20 Immeasurably long period of time (4)

22 Blighty (7)

23 Customers (5)

24 Schoolchildren who return to an empty home (8,4)

DOWN

2 Involve (someone) in a dispute (7)

3 Unit of power — Scottish engineer, d. 1819 (4)

4 Stretch out (6)

5 Deadly (8)

6 North American elk (5)

7 Isolation (of a hermit?) (12)

8 Assume control of a situation (4,3,5)

13 Hand down (8)

16 Make believe (7)

17 Coastal department of western France (6)

19 Illumination (5)

21 Perform in the street for money (4)

Solution see page 242

40

ACROSS

1 Annoying (10)

7 Exploded (5,2)

8 Asian country (5)

10 A lot (4)

11 Offer of marriage (8)

13 Noon (6)

15 (Draw with) a coloured stick (6)

17 Go into the red (8)

18 Swear (4)

21 Rope-making fibre (5)

22 Wild mountain sheep of Corsica — mono flu (anag) (7)

23 Two-story flat (10)

DOWN

1 Former PM (5)

2 Diminutive (4)

3 Run out (6)

4 Indoor footwear (8)

5 Self-deprecating quality (7)

6 Self-denying (10)

9 Omniscient (3–7)

12 Father of Icarus (8)

14 Taking place far from land (4–3)

16 (Now mainly farmed) fish (6)

19 Worth (5)

20 Kick — bet — boat (4)

Solution see page 242

41

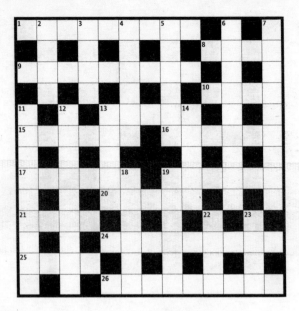

ACROSS

1 Savagery (9)
8 Well I never! (4)
9 Shut up shop (5,4)
10 Flog (4)
13 Peculiar (5)
15 One of the Twelve Apostles (6)
16 Cowardly (6)
17 Northern girls? (6)
19 Pieces (6)
20 Light theatrical entertainment (5)
21 Incline (4)
24 Italian restaurant (9)
25 Rabbit (4)
26 Names of the most promising applicants for a job, selected for further consideration (9)

DOWN

2 Part in a play (4)
3 Audition (4)
4 Convenience (6)
5 Showy without taste or worth (6)
6 Let the cat out of the bag (4,5)
7 Cover-up — wall coating (9)
11 Sports — cheat list (anag) (9)
12 Seaboard (9)
13 Adam's ale (5)
14 Two in cards or dice (5)
18 Look for (6)
19 It's our (anag) — admirer (6)
22 Play tenpins (4)
23 X (4)

Solution see page 243

42

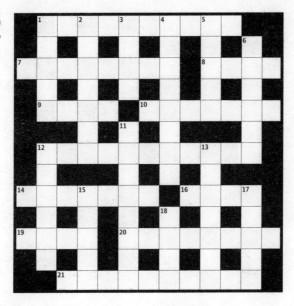

ACROSS

1 Contrived (10)
7 Something made out of a molehill? (8)
8 Furnished holiday house in France (4)
9 Gardener's basket (4)
10 Espied (7)
12 Old county of north-west England (11)
14 Area with fruit trees (7)
16 Run smoothly (4)
19 Lacking sparkle (4)
20 Wizard (8)
21 On the face of it (10)

DOWN

1 To great height (5)
2 Languages (7)
3 Anti-aircraft fire (4)
4 Plot (8)
5 Acute, but unspecific, feeling of anxiety (5)
6 Be present (6)
11 Food of the gods (8)
12 In a cautious manner (6)
13 Malady (7)
15 Angry — agitated (3,2)
17 Tearful (5)
18 Unencumbered (4)

Solution see page 243

43

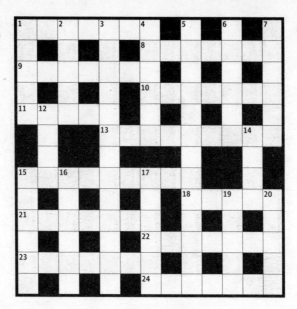

ACROSS

1 Small dried seedless grape (7)
8 Meatier (anag) — Qatar, for example (7)
9 Deficiency of red blood cells (7)
10 Globes (7)
11 Stinking (5)
13 Without doubt (9)
15 Declared to be a saint (9)
18 Roughage (5)
21 Hormone produced in the pancreas (7)
22 Copy (7)
23 One of Harpo's brothers (7)
24 Mischievousness — rascally tricks (7)

DOWN

1 Banter — corn husks (5)
2 Cook in an oven (5)
3 War (5,8)
4 Tricky question (6)
5 Scottish dance (8,5)
6 French president (6)
7 Liverpool's river (6)
12 __ Pound, American poet (4)
14 Shakespearean king (4)
15 Cower (6)
16 One who fails to arrive (2-4)
17 Elder (6)
19 Courageous (5)
20 Adversary (5)

Solution see page 243

44

ACROSS

1 Raw cured Italian ham (10)
7 Heartfelt (7)
8 Buckwheat pancakes (5)
10 Gosh! (1,3)
11 Capital of Bosnia and Herzegovina (8)
13 Deeply distressing (6)
15 Decapitate (6)
17 Item of jewellery (8)
18 Complain (4)
21 DVD player button (5)
22 Vertical (7)
23 Evaluation (10)

DOWN

1 Black-and-white bear (5)
2 Sign of things to come (4)
3 Of the same period — alcove (anag) (6)
4 Impartial (8)
5 Ancient vessel with three banks of oars on each side (7)
6 Aid (10)
9 Excessive (10)
12 Charlotte Brontë novel (8)
14 Toxophilites (7)
16 Clothing worn in an operating theatre (6)
19 Should (5)
20 Veracious (4)

Solution see page 243

45

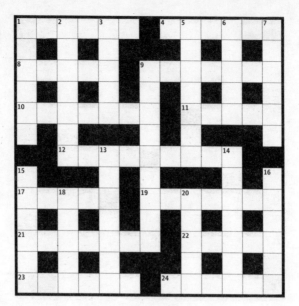

ACROSS

1 Given often to poor health (6)
4 Writhe (6)
8 Ground meat (5)
9 Upper limit (7)
10 Someone else (7)
11 Dodge (5)
12 Behave in a silly way (4,5)
17 Come clean (3,2)
19 Edible fungus — chocolate sweet (7)
21 A derisory amount of money (7)
22 Lock of hair (5)
23 Cleaning cloth (6)
24 Fleet of ships (6)

DOWN

1 Ape-like (6)
2 Toe the line (7)
3 Blood-sucking worm (5)
5 Indeed (5,2)
6 One of the Balearic Islands (5)
7 Lodestone, for example (6)
9 Don Quixote author (9)
13 Catch (7)
14 Fabric — a fat eft (anag) (7)
15 Lethargic (6)
16 Iran, formerly (6)
18 Less than average tidal rises and falls (5)
20 Speak (5)

Solution see page 244

46

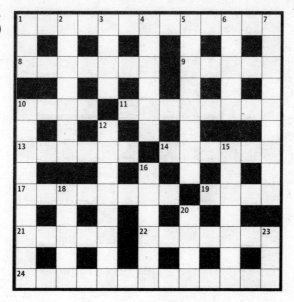

ACROSS

1 Stealthy (13)
8 Lattice (anag) (7)
9 River of forgetfulness (5)
10 Inflamed swelling (4)
11 Precious metal (8)
13 Havoc (6)
14 Shut (6)
17 Strong drive for success (8)
19 Short extract from a film (4)
21 Poisonous (5)
22 Broadcasts — exposures (7)
24 Overdo (something) (5,2,6)

DOWN

1 Solidified (3)
2 Put right (7)
3 Surpassing the ordinary (4)
4 Threefold — singing voice (6)
5 Sneak (8)
6 Choose to participate (3,2)
7 Indignant (7,2)
10 Pompous — inflated (9)
12 US state, capital Frankfort (8)
15 Absence of sound (7)
16 Independent principality on the French Riviera (6)
18 Pugilist (5)
20 Most important point (4)
23 Little sibling (3)

Solution see page 244

47

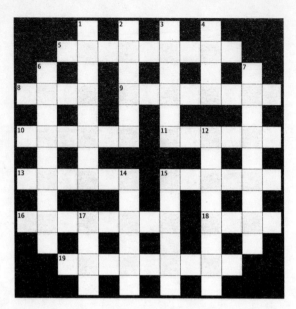

ACROSS

5 Event in which a baton is passed (5,4)

8 Chops, steaks etc (4)

9 Verdict (8)

10 Saunter in no particular direction (6)

11 Fountainhead — journalist's informant (6)

13 Metal workers (6)

15 With circumspection (6)

16 Woollen garments (8)

18 Hide — flay (4)

19 Flowing slowly (9)

DOWN

1 Principal ingredient of borscht (8)

2 Water Music composer, d. 1759 (6)

3 Noisy quarrel (6)

4 Cold refreshments (4)

6 Evidence (9)

7 Fine ceramic ware (9)

12 Revolt (8)

14 Horrible smell (6)

15 Trill (6)

17 Legal wrong (4)

Solution see page 244

48

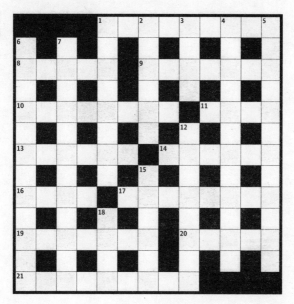

ACROSS

1 Something beyond criticism (6,3)
8 Vietnamese capital (5)
9 Helper or attendant (sometimes humble or obedient?) (7)
10 Render motionless (8)
11 Emperor (4)
13 Short-sighted (6)
14 Old mercantile area of Venice (6)
16 Emperor (who fiddled while Rome burned?) d. AD68 (4)
17 Seed of a palm chewed (with its leaves) as a narcotic (5,3)
19 Judge (7)
20 Round Dutch cheese (5)
21 Pine, for example (9)

DOWN

1 Outfit for a dip (8)
2 Sweet blackcurrant liqueur (6)
3 Get by working (4)
4 Sofa for reclining on (6,6)
5 Carnivorous aquatic bug (5,7)
6 Composite picture (12)
7 Ominous — critical (12)
12 Professional killer (5,3)
15 Order (6)
18 Stockmarket operator gambling on a quick profit (4)

Solution see page 244

49

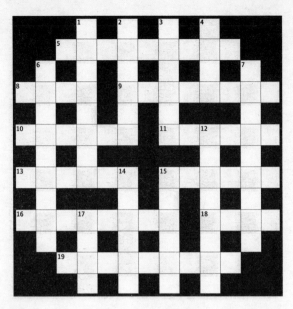

ACROSS

5 Limit (9)

8 Tiller (4)

9 Take more reservations than there are places available (8)

10 Orange vegetable (6)

11 Make certain for the future (6)

13 I am grateful (6)

15 Amalgamation (6)

16 Valiant and chivalrous (8)

18 Travelling bag (4)

19 Awkward (9)

DOWN

1 'Deafening silence', for example — or on my ox (anag) (8)

2 Come off the booze (3,3)

3 Unit of electric current (6)

4 Sudden sharp feeling (4)

6 Voice-amplifying device (9)

7 Middle-class (9)

12 Harem — or silage (anag) (8)

14 Device for finding one's way (6)

15 Town officials (6)

17 Butting animal (4)

Solution see page 245

50

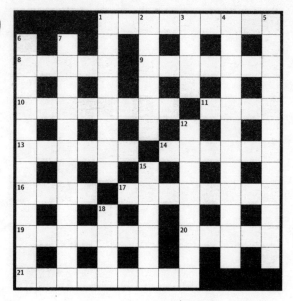

ACROSS

1 Kitchen utensil (4,5)
8 Behave theatrically (5)
9 One with personal attractiveness (7)
10 Person kept in custody (8)
11 Brandenburg Concertos composer, d. 1750 (4)
13 Simpleton — pasta (6)
14 Bad-tempered complainant (6)
16 Place for keeping racing pigeons (4)
17 Group of rowdy young American film stars of the 1980s (4,4)
19 Leaves the house (4,3)
20 Gallery for works of art — loans (anag) (5)
21 Alternate (4,5)

DOWN

1 Pliant (8)
2 Small soft container — a chest (anag) (6)
3 Mop (4)
4 Limitless (12)
5 Of seismic proportions (5–7)
6 Influential member (7,5)
7 One with a compulsive desire to manipulate others (7,5)
12 Raises objection (8)
15 Kitchen utensil (6)
18 Outer garment (4)

Solution see page 245

51

ACROSS

1 Vehicle carrying a ladder and hoses (4,6)

7 Filmed scene that ends on the cutting-room floor (7)

8 Old church tax (5)

10 Dip in liquid (4)

11 In a careless manner (8)

13 Attacker (6)

15 Convenient (6)

17 Thawed (8)

18 Begin to move (4)

21 Comedy of the absurd? (5)

22 Three-pronged spear (7)

23 Where glass containers can be recycled (6,4)

DOWN

1 Kind of mattress (5)

2 Horse with reddish-brown coat (4)

3 Uniformly (6)

4 Support for a hinged barrier (8)

5 Absolutely! (3,4)

6 Cosmetic pad (6,4)

9 Thrill (10)

12 Evocative (8)

14 Great fire (7)

16 Grinding tool (6)

19 Make minor adjustments (5)

20 Oral examination (4)

Solution see page 245

52

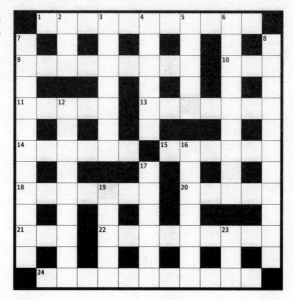

ACROSS

1 Remain south (anag) — migratory bird (5,6)
9 Forerunner (9)
10 Sound made by a pigeon (3)
11 Dusk to dawn (5)
13 Purported (7)
14 Hostelry (6)
15 Pounce — pogo stick part (6)
18 Meander (anag) (7)
20 Drink alcohol (5)
21 Not many (3)
22 Shopping by post (4,5)
24 Striking (3-8)

DOWN

2 Half and half? (3)
3 Stroll (7)
4 Foreign intelligence agency (6)
5 Relating to the countryside (5)
6 With one's identity concealed (9)
7 Wastrel (11)
8 Fictitious name (3,2,6)
12 Yielding (6,3)
16 Bagpipe music (7)
17 Junkie (6)
19 Ape (5)
23 Loud noise (3)

Solution see page 245

53

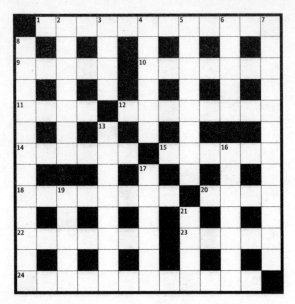

ACROSS

1 Heart specialist (12)
9 Lifeless (5)
10 Cases (7)
11 Yanks (4)
12 Intermittently (2,3,3)
14 Extreme fear (6)
15 To an equal extent (2,4)
18 Cures (8)
20 Star Wars warrior (4)
22 Minty sweets (7)
23 Roosting place (5)
24 Commendable (12)

DOWN

2 One who retaliates — engrave (anag) (7)
3 Show excessive affection (4)
4 Accessible via the internet (6)
5 Cathedral musician (8)
6 Its state capital is Boise (5)
7 Shakespeare play (7,5)
8 Totalitarian regime (12)
13 State of inactivity or stagnation (8)
16 Dig up (7)
17 Playground item (6)
19 Venomous African snake (5)
21 Stimulus (4)

Solution see page 246

54

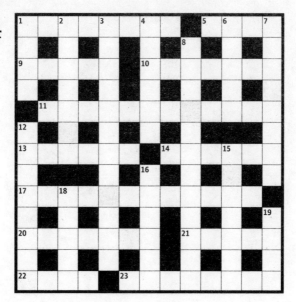

ACROSS

1 Girl's name — a sorry me! (anag) (8)
5 Sharp sound of disapproval (4)
9 Natural aptitude (5)
10 Fishing vessel (7)
11 Stamina — endurance (7,5)
13 Russian wolfhound (6)
14 Confederates (6)
17 Close shave (6,6)
20 The Gunners (7)
21 Drug used to treat Parkinson's disease (1-4)
22 River running through Newcastle (4)
23 Trinket — decoration (8)

DOWN

1 Prevalent (4)
2 First course (7)
3 Fairground ride (5-2-5)
4 Non-commissioned sailor in the Royal Navy (6)
6 Relative by marriage (2-3)
7 Something unexpected (8)
8 Dry red Italian wine (12)
12 Plentiful (8)
15 Collapse inwards (7)
16 Kitchen gadget — old policeman (6)
18 Sticky substance exuded by pine trees (5)
19 Breathe noisily after running (4)

Solution see page 246

55

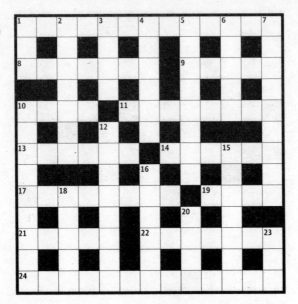

ACROSS

1 One who fails to hold a catch (13)
8 Gods (7)
9 Make fun of (5)
10 Fuel (4)
11 Infatuated (8)
13 Prescribed ceremony (6)
14 Very weak (6)
17 New Year's Eve for Scots (8)
19 Gold-coloured (4)
21 Growl viciously (5)
22 Panther (7)
24 Conceited (7–6)

DOWN

1 Offer a price (3)
2 Dense shrubbery (7)
3 Morally wrong (4)
4 Decay (6)
5 Main element of air (8)
6 Perform (5)
7 Best-balanced — it's sedate (anag) (9)
10 Liver disease (9)
12 Imaginary line round the Earth (8)
15 Robber — darn big (anag) (7)
16 Large oceanic sport fish (6)
18 Seabird excrement, once prized as fertiliser (5)
20 Circular pyramid (4)
23 Broken (3)

Solution see page 246

56

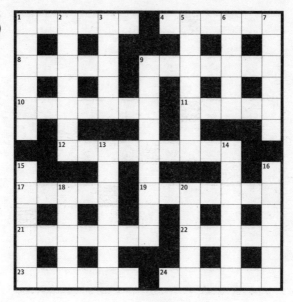

ACROSS

1 Huggable (6)
4 Turned — malodorous (6)
8 Above the horizon (5)
9 Absurd pretence (7)
10 Supervise (7)
11 Impossible (3,2)
12 Awarded medals (9)
17 Criminal (5)
19 European Union's most southerly capital (7)
21 Educational institution (7)
22 Tartan cloth (5)
23 Herb tea (6)
24 Trapped (6)

DOWN

1 Incentive (6)
2 Bloat (7)
3 Golf course by the sea (5)
5 Opposing (7)
6 Repeated rhythmic phrase (5)
7 (Spanish) chaperone (6)
9 Intervening space (9)
13 Institutional eating place (7)
14 Hopelessness (7)
15 Remnant (6)
16 Praised (6)
18 Sprawls (5)
20 Castrated chicken (5)

Solution see page 246

57

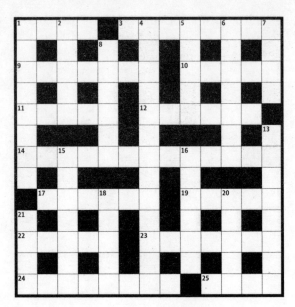

ACROSS

1 American tramp (4)
3 Area covered with trees (8)
9 Fascinate (7)
10 Very bright (5)
11 Ryan O'Neal's actress daughter (5)
12 Rigid support for a broken bone (6)
14 On the other hand (13)
17 Barista's product (6)
19 ___ da Gama, Portuguese explorer, d. 1524 (5)
22 Garment — period of work (5)
23 Aged (7)
24 Ponder (8)
25 Siegfried and Tristan Farnon, for example (4)

DOWN

1 Customary (8)
2 Large broad bay — middle part of a slack rope (5)
4 Exaggeration (13)
5 Demon (5)
6 Move forward (7)
7 Lower part of an interior wall (4)
8 Cook just below boiling point (6)
13 Words with the same meaning (8)
15 Radioactive element — rout him (anag) (7)
16 Overrun (6)
18 Belong (3,2)
20 Carefree and lively outing (5)
21 Person taking drugs (4)

Solution see page 247

58

ACROSS

1 Appraise (6)
4 High terrain (5)
7 Cream cake (6)
8 Small inexpensive eatery (6)
9 Bide one's time (4)
10 Excessively fond of drink (8)
12 Hiding (11)
17 Gemstone (8)
19 Religious ceremony (4)
20 (Of food) necessary and important (6)
21 Rue (6)
22 Bad-tempered and unfriendly (5)
23 With pleasure (6)

DOWN

1 Antiquated (7)
2 Austere — like Lysander? (7)
3 Area where bushes are planted (9)
4 Japanese verse form (5)
5 Disappointed (3,4)
6 Liverpudlian (6)
11 Two-sided (9)
13 Alfresco (4-3)
14 Very angry (7)
15 Unsteady on one's feet (7)
16 Gives rise to — crusades (6)
18 Yuletide greenery (5)

Solution see page 247

59

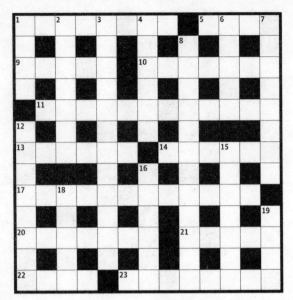

ACROSS

1 Diminutive folk hero (3,5)

5 Serious break in friendly relations (4)

9 From the Italian capital (5)

10 Mobster (7)

11 16th-century Spanish adventurer (12)

13 Warm up again (6)

14 Keen insight (6)

17 One way to leave a pirate ship for ever? (4,3,5)

20 Vibrating membrane in the head (7)

21 Regular (5)

22 Bluish shade of green (4)

23 Lineage (8)

DOWN

1 Sour — acid (4)

2 Enormous (7)

3 Animal's rear (12)

4 Fabric made with angora wool (6)

6 Did little or nothing (5)

7 Large tropical seedpod with tangy pulp — mad train (anag) (8)

8 Gardening (12)

12 Bully (8)

15 Search for a fugitive (7)

16 Dirty rats? (6)

18 Insect's feeding stage (5)

19 Have fun — theatrical work (4)

Solution see page 247

60

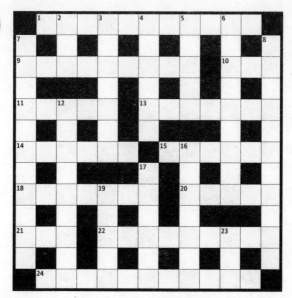

ACROSS

1 Extended built-up area (11)
9 I have no idea! (4,3,2)
10 Storage container (3)
11 Easily understood (5)
13 Section (anag) — spots (7)
14 Broken pieces of pottery (6)
15 Disappear (6)
18 Blow up (7)
20 Inexpensive (5)
21 Label — children's game (3)
22 Prestigious group of US universities (3,6)
24 Waterproof boots (11)

DOWN

2 Acknowledge (3)
3 Without assistance (7)
4 Skimpy bathing costume (6)
5 Larceny (5)
6 Aim (9)
7 Young people (11)
8 Chirping insect (11)
12 Sparkling wine (9)
16 Very old (7)
17 Native of Nairobi, perhaps (6)
19 Projecting bay window — Oxford college (5)
23 Information (3)

Solution see page 247

61

ACROSS

5 Eve of All Saints' Day (9)
8 Girl (of Richmond Hill?) (4)
9 Tea party — official function — heated argument (8)
10 Whine tearfully (6)
11 Annually (6)
13 Looked fixedly (6)
15 Small wave (6)
16 Homeric wanderer (8)
18 Sliding window frame (4)
19 Short work of fiction (9)

DOWN

1 Jewish festival celebrated in March or April (8)
2 Worldwide (6)
3 A score (6)
4 Fairy of Persian folklore (4)
6 Size (9)
7 Without offspring (9)
12 Relevant (8)
14 More profound (6)
15 Duty list (6)
17 (Fruit of the) blackthorn (4)

Solution see page 248

62

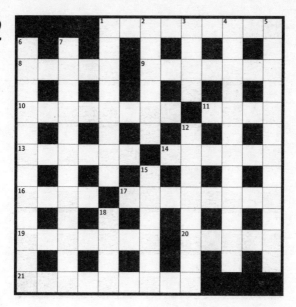

ACROSS

1 Small restaurant (9)

8 Residential building (5)

9 Ancient burial mound (7)

10 Sound right (4,4)

11 Apple's virtual assistant (4)

13 Large containers for milk (6)

14 Swollen — drug it (anag) (6)

16 Options available (4)

17 Light flat Italian bread (8)

19 Greek vowel (7)

20 West African capital (5)

21 Time of youth and inexperience (5,4)

DOWN

1 Tangible (anag) — animal noise (8)

2 Legendary British king (6)

3 Amounts of money (4)

4 Railway vehicles (7,5)

5 Old trading ship (4,8)

6 Meagre rations (5,7)

7 Recurring every five years (12)

12 Objects of dread or apprehension (8)

15 Capital on the Danube (6)

18 Power distribution network (4)

Solution see page 248

63

ACROSS

1 Film or book making huge profits (11)

9 Staying power (9)

10 Yellowish-brown (3)

11 See how the land lies (informal) (5)

13 Put in order — organise (7)

14 The man (anag) — uplifting song (6)

15 Intellectual capacity (6)

18 Can be upheld (7)

20 Groom (oneself) with evident vanity (5)

21 Mongrel (3)

22 Volume of liquid used in cooking (9)

24 Has an unhappy outcome (4,2,5)

DOWN

2 Boy (3)

3 Funeral procession (7)

4 Author of Pilgrim's Progress, d.1688 (6)

5 Remove fleece (5)

6 Far-reaching (9)

7 Coronary (5,6)

8 All the time (11)

12 Make a rapid escape (3,3,3)

16 Ecstasy (7)

17 Take into custody (6)

19 Public swimming pool (5)

23 Distant (3)

Solution see page 248

64

ACROSS

1 Member of a Christian group that worships enthusiastically (5-6)
9 Baby's discomfort (5,4)
10 Impair (3)
11 Force out (5)
13 Very small fish that burrows into beaches (4,3)
14 Yikes, I've dropped something! (6)
15 Bailey's circus partner, d. 1891 (6)
18 Cold summer drink (4,3)
20 High-tension power line support (5)
21 Peter Nissen's ubiquitous structure (3)
22 Play the field (9)
24 Various bits (4,3,4)

DOWN

2 Device making sound louder (3)
3 Record of wages earned (3,4)
4 Section of legal document (6)
5 Anaemic looking (5)
6 Small plant with creeping stems, sometimes scarlet (9)
7 Too thin? (11)
8 Initial (11)
12 Sheltered (9)
16 Resting serenely (2,5)
17 State (6)
19 Sorts (5)
23 Pa (3)

Solution see page 248

65

ACROSS

1 Categorise (10)
7 Cloudy (8)
8 White tissue under the rind of citrus fruit (4)
9 Profound (4)
10 Liberty (7)
12 Bestir oneself (3,8)
14 Beetroot soup (7)
16 Closed (4)
19 Mountain lion (4)
20 People from Birmingham (8)
21 Marry (3,3,4)

DOWN

1 Covered with a firm surface (5)
2 Article of clothing (7)
3 Spoken (4)
4 Threefold feat (3,5)
5 Oversight (5)
6 Powerful (6)
11 Ban (8)
12 Become an adult (4,2)
13 Brutal (7)
15 Citizen of a landlocked monarchy in southern Africa (5)
17 Message from Trump? (5)
18 Proverbially stubborn beast (4)

Solution see page 249

66

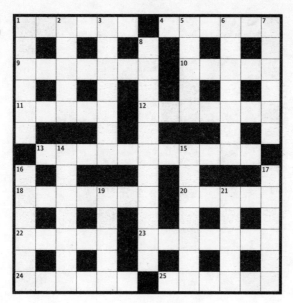

ACROSS

1 College finance officer (6)
4 Saggy (6)
9 Mark made under a 'c' (7)
10 Rubbish — underwear (5)
11 Stratum (5)
12 Diamond shape (7)
13 Whatever happens (4,4,3)
18 Brief break (7)
20 Condition added to something already agreed (5)
22 Confused (2,3)
23 Feed (7)
24 Solution (6)
25 Insincerely emotional — like cheddar? (6)

DOWN

1 Bend out of shape (6)
2 Rosy (5)
3 Free (2,5)
5 Highest capital city in South America (2,3)
6 Source of great wealth (7)
7 Votes in favour (6)
8 Take charge in making a decision (4,3,4)
14 Process of unconscious assimilation (7)
15 Via (7)
16 Layers (6)
17 In a sly manner (6)
19 Speak (5)
21 Chauffeur — force (5)

Solution see page 249

67

ACROSS

5 Improved (11)

7 Underground storage organ for some plants (4)

8 Lethargic (8)

9 With a rigid manner (7)

11 Ballroom dance originally from Germany (5)

13 Car crash (5)

14 English plume (de ma tante?) (7)

16 Be noticeable (5,3)

17 Cook in hot water (4)

18 Perceptiveness — good taste (11)

DOWN

1 Pavement edge (4)

2 Small cake of deep-fried minced meat (7)

3 Haughty (5)

4 Not circulating or flowing (8)

5 Polluted (11)

6 Spread malicious gossip (informal) (4,3,4)

10 Liking (for something) (8)

12 Roman god of the sea (7)

15 Brassed off (5)

17 Meat — complaint (4)

Solution see page 249

68

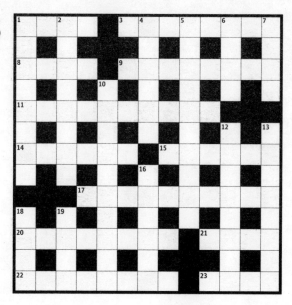

ACROSS

1 Corpse (4)

3 Widespread outbreak of disease (8)

8 Twilight (4)

9 Capital city on the Danube (8)

11 Teenage (10)

14 Uniform — suffering from gastric distress (6)

15 Prolonged distressing experience (6)

17 Railing at the side of a balcony (10)

20 The Granite City (8)

21 Front of the leg below the knee (4)

22 Benevolence (8)

23 Nervous (4)

DOWN

1 Easily influenced (8)

2 Go into solution (8)

4 Deliver a sermon (6)

5 Debauched (10)

6 Honey-based drink (4)

7 Symbol written on sheet music to indicate pitch (4)

10 Scene of uproar and confusion (4,6)

12 Unconnected (8)

13 Third largest of the Channel Islands (8)

16 Coercion (6)

18 Fire — bag (4)

19 Enthusiastic (4)

Solution see page 249

69

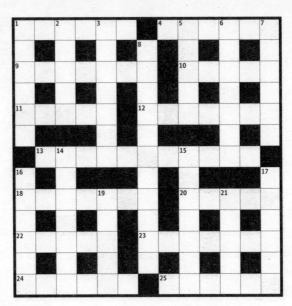

ACROSS

1 Remove weapons from (6)

4 Large — universal (6)

9 Sturdy 'British' dog (7)

10 Fed up (5)

11 Staunch (5)

12 Undergoing court process (2,5)

13 Dinner jacket worn with a white shirt (informal) (7,4)

18 Kenyan capital (7)

20 Irk (5)

22 Perch (5)

23 Anger at having been offended (7)

24 Work by Keats or Shelley, say (6)

25 Breathe out (6)

DOWN

1 Try something briefly and superficially (6)

2 Preposterous (5)

3 Sign of danger (or socialism)? (3,4)

5 Path around (5)

6 Gin and vermouth (7)

7 Hold close, affectionately (6)

8 Humiliating (11)

14 Embodiment (7)

15 Crate used by orators at Speakers' Corner? (7)

16 Deceive — lead on (6)

17 Painted or sculpted band running round under the ceiling (6)

19 External (5)

21 Tropical fruit with yellow skin and pink pulp (5)

Solution see page 250

70

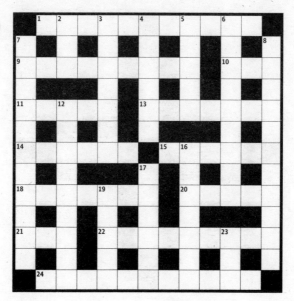

ACROSS

1 Peanut scale (anag) — put in concise form (11)

9 For the most part (2,3,4)

10 Type of bread (3)

11 Dog (5)

13 Rich tea, for example (7)

14 Hinder (6)

15 Goblin, elf or imp (6)

18 Largest living primate (7)

20 Shafted weapon for throwing or thrusting (5)

21 Tax-free savings account (3)

22 Newly coined word (9)

24 Famous people (11)

DOWN

2 Muggins (3)

3 Rectified (7)

4 Despicable — BBC, say (anag) (6)

5 Respiratory organs (5)

6 Greenish blue (9)

7 In good physical condition (8,3)

8 Timpani (11)

12 Capital letters (5,4)

16 Faint — finish military training (4,3))

17 Toil (6)

19 Shafted weapon used on horseback (5)

23 Choler (3)

71

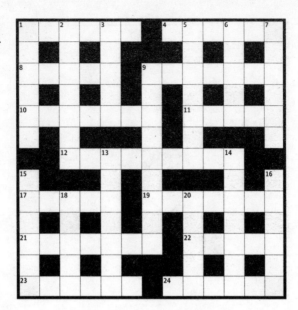

ACROSS

1 Remove by applying friction (3,3)
4 Fiery and passionate (6)
8 Same as above (5)
9 Furry pet (7)
10 Bag — latches (anag) (7)
11 Vamp (5)
12 Please do! (2,2,5)
17 Mortal (5)
19 Robot resembling 17 (7)
21 Swimmer's breathing tube (7)
22 Floral leaf (5)
23 Prayer beads (6)
24 Sculpted (6)

DOWN

1 Hottish salad plant (6)
2 American body-washing facility (7)
3 Foam (5)
5 All together (2,5)
6 Elector (5)
7 Bold (6)
9 Go, Hillary! (anag) — chalice used by Jesus at the Last Supper (4,5)
13 Nickname (7)
14 Ballroom dance (3-4)
15 Beer after whisky, say (or vice versa) (6)
16 (Of an egg) went bad (6)
18 Open heathlands (5)
20 Profundity (5)

Solution see page 250

72

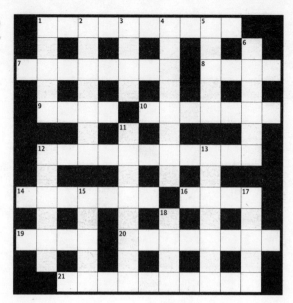

ACROSS

1 American car (10)
7 Wanting someone else's advantages (8)
8 Neat (4)
9 Prominence (4)
10 Bloodshed (7)
12 High bar jumper (4-7)
14 One-horned creature (7)
16 Expectorate (4)
19 Sympathy for others (4)
20 Traditional Cypriot cheese (8)
21 Top catwalk strutter (10)

DOWN

1 Distant (5)
2 Designed to protect from cold (7)
3 Tie up a boat (4)
4 Give it everything (4,1,3)
5 Grant entry (3,2)
6 Orange-brown (6)
11 Galosh (8)
12 HB writer? (6)
13 Walked as quietly as possible (7)
15 (Fur of) a South American rodent (5)
17 An official language of Sri Lanka (5)
18 Hit hard (4)

Solution see page 250

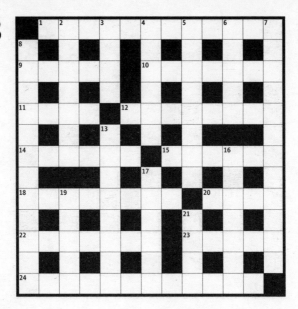

ACROSS

1 Intensely painful (12)
9 Kingdom (5)
10 Streamlined cover for an aircraft engine (7)
11 Domestic animals (4)
12 Tyrannical (8)
14 Non-metallic element found in all organic compounds (6)
15 Rarely (6)
18 Killer (8)
20 Spill the beans (4)
22 Eyelet lining a small hole (7)
23 Blacksmith's block (5)
24 Place of detention for those awaiting trial (6,6)

DOWN

2 Noteworthy special quality (1-6)
3 Play boisterously (4)
4 Curved outwards (6)
5 Conventional — customary (8)
6 Opening through which fluid can pass (5)
7 Rhinestone Cowboy singer (4,8)
8 Say something very embarrassing (4,1,7)
13 Riders (8)
16 Rescue (7)
17 Relating to living organisms (6)
19 Violent weather (5)
21 German writer concerned with the role of the artist in society, d. 1955 (4)

74

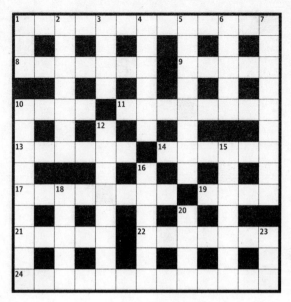

ACROSS

1 Providing double security (4,3,6)
8 Farm vehicle (7)
9 Hold firmly (5)
10 Brewery product (4)
11 Rotary (8)
13 London rail terminus (6)
14 Deft (6)
17 Courgette (8)
19 South African currency (4)
21 Major's successor as PM (5)
22 Experienced sailors? (3,4)
24 Refrain from talking (6,4,3)

DOWN

1 Binary digit (3)
2 Several (anag) — Brexiteers (7)
3 Play parts (4)
4 Author of The Descent of Man (6)
5 Killer of a king (8)
6 Go on all fours (5)
7 Distinguished — divided (9)
10 Prince of Darkness (9)
12 Philanderer (8)
15 Enjoying a winning streak (2,1,4)
16 International agency — no cues (anag) (6)
18 Nautical map (5)
20 Hamlet was one (4)
23 Fluid in a plant (3)

Solution see page 251

75

ACROSS

1 Art of good eating (10)

7 Expressing poetic sorrow for something past (7)

8 American stock farm (5)

10 Form on which a shoe is made (4)

11 Even more snobby (8)

13 Canopy over a four-poster bed (6)

15 Woman's dress in Tyrolean style (6)

17 Postscript to a literary work (8)

18 In excited eagerness (4)

21 Hindu male religious teacher (5)

22 Traders — leaders (anag) (7)

23 Titular university head (10)

DOWN

1 Speculation (5)

2 Mistake — small piece of paper (4)

3 Running fast (6)

4 Unconsciousness induced by drugs (8)

5 Large house (7)

6 Gets rid of unnecessary jumble (10)

9 Maker of timepieces (10)

12 Strong emotional attachment (8)

14 Popeye the Sailor's vegetable of choice (7)

16 Go bad — turn from liquid into solids (6)

19 Author of The Female Eunuch, b.1939 (5)

20 Lament noisily (4)

Solution see page 251

76

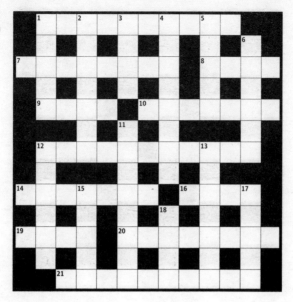

ACROSS

1 Duke of 21's horse at Waterloo — capital city (10)

7 Parts of speech — poor nuns (anag) (8)

8 Greek aniseed liqueur (4)

9 Arrangement for deferred payment (4)

10 Unpaid debts (7)

12 Capital city — uneasier sob (anag) (6,5)

14 Interminable (7)

16 Habitual drunk (4)

19 Bonce (4)

20 Extremely agitated — if recent (anag) (8)

21 Kind of boot (10)

DOWN

1 French landscape painter, d. 1875 (5)

2 Flamboyant style (7)

3 Common sense (4)

4 Hitler's nationality pre-1925 (8)

5 Bring to mind (5)

6 Portuguese North Atlantic islands (6)

11 Swollen-headed (8)

12 Decrepit old car (6)

13 Minaret (anag) — clothing (7)

15 Provide accommodation for (5)

17 Pungent vegetable (5)

18 Penny-pinching (4)

Solution see page 251

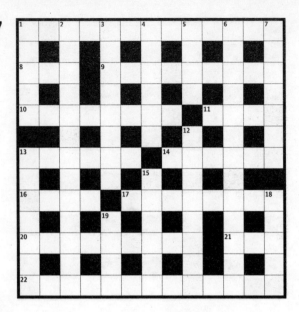

ACROSS

1 The Rastafarian Messiah (5,8)

8 Crazy (3)

9 Scotch pancake (4,5)

10 Exhume (8)

11 Sister and wife of Zeus (4)

13 Golfer who can't drive straight? (6)

14 Author of Little Women, d. 1888 (6)

16 Hard work (4)

17 Large German dirigible (8)

20 Leader (9)

21 Metal, Sn (3)

22 Person with whom one shares common attitudes (7,6)

DOWN

1 Moist (5)

2 Illness (13)

3 Put at risk (8)

4 Recalled (6)

5 Peas (anag) — part of a church (4)

6 Eventually (6,2,5)

7 Handsome (7)

12 Flimsy sandal (4–4)

13 Use any office workstation, not having a permanent one (3–4)

15 Running late (6)

18 Composition for nine instruments (5)

19 Morose (4)

78

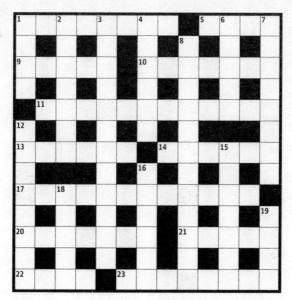

ACROSS

1 Opinion sampler (8)
5 Sound of a heavy fall (4)
9 Scoundrel (5)
10 Igneous rock (7)
11 Cats in litter (anag) — woodwind player (12)
13 Bereft child (6)
14 Something unique (3-3)
17 Forever (2,10)
20 Hazel nut (7)
21 Abnormally active (5)
22 Gather a crop (4)
23 Resinous (anag) — unspecific personality disturbance (8)

DOWN

1 After-dinner wine (4)
2 Fielding position (3,4)
3 Extra on stage as part of a crowd scene (5,7)
4 Locomotive (6)
6 Caribbean country (5)
7 Colouring substance (8)
8 German Protestant theologian, d. 1546 (6,6)
12 Highly desirable or alluring (2,3,3)
15 Eight-limbed cephalopod (7)
16 Soft and soothing (6)
18 Lively dance, originally from Bohemia (5)
19 Bauxite, haematite etc (4)

Solution see page 252

79

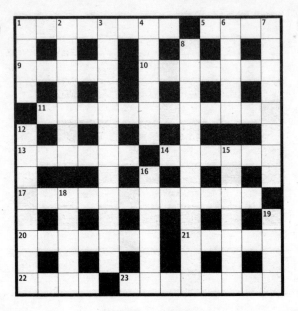

ACROSS

1 Ear membrane — my MP a nut (anag) (8)
5 Sudden sharp feeling (4)
9 Tycoon — ski slope mound (5)
10 Gulf sheikhdom (7)
11 Grouchy (12)
13 Expresses audibly (6)
14 Calm (6)
17 Dinosaur with a long neck and tail (12)
20 In the open air (7)
21 Dirty (5)
22 Boot (4)
23 No 1 in the periodic table (8)

DOWN

1 Hours clocked up? (4)
2 Person moving abroad (7)
3 Poetic rhyming device using words with the same initial letter (12)
4 Cultured (6)
6 Where Davy Crockett died, 1836 (5)
7 Hoodlum (8)
8 Fast food — begs cure here (anag) (12)
12 Skin cream to filter out ultraviolet light (8)
15 Droll (7)
16 Up the garden path? (6)
18 Device for measuring out spirits (5)
19 Bluish green (4)

Solution see page 252

80

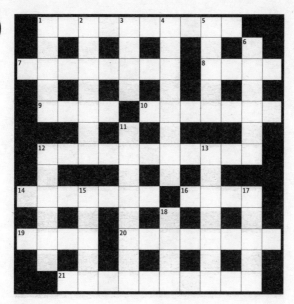

ACROSS

1 Carefully thought out (10)
7 Long-sleeved glove (8)
8 Rolled tortilla with a filling (4)
9 Obligation (4)
10 (Make a) gross mistake (7)
12 Wary and unwilling to take risks (11)
14 Disproportionately long and slender (7)
16 One-sided inclination (4)
19 Stretch of open land covered with heather and bracken (4)
20 Grasp (4,4)
21 Restored to a former position (10)

DOWN

1 7th-century BC Athenian whose law code imposed death for even trivial offences (5)
2 Weariness (7)
3 Papal edict (4)
4 Hustlers (anag) — like 1 down? (8)
5 Saturn's largest satellite (5)
6 Consent to receive (6)
11 Short official statement (8)
12 One who hunts down and confines another (6)
13 Descriptive word or phrase (7)
15 Audacity (informal) (5)
17 Dish of raw vegetables (5)
18 Satirical sketch (4)

Solution see page 252

81

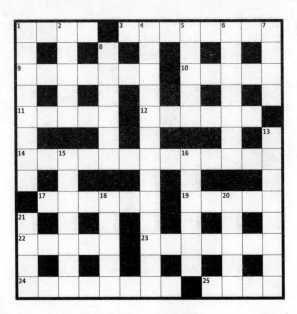

ACROSS

1 Notable achievement (4)

3 Happening irregularly (8)

9 Correctly reasoned (7)

10 Junket — children's comic (5)

11 Public assembly for open discussion (5)

12 Biblical heroine, who married the king of Persia (6)

14 Executive (13)

17 Sausage (6)

19 Girl (sometimes lazy?) (5)

22 Equivocate (5)

23 Almost certainly (2,5)

24 Absence of light (8)

25 Vigil — wash (4)

DOWN

1 Fail completely (4,4)

2 One of the seven deadly sins (5)

4 Influenced or controlled deviously (6,7)

5 Capital of Morocco (5)

6 Loved one (7)

7 Henhouse (4)

8 Eugene O'Neill's figure of 'death' (the one who cometh!) (6)

13 Girl with dark brown hair (8)

15 Wander aimlessly (7)

16 Make one's home permanently (6)

18 Pick up information (5)

20 Steam bath (5)

21 Landlocked desert country of northern central Africa, formerly a French colony (4)

Solution see page 253

82

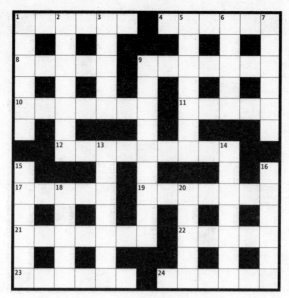

ACROSS

1 Artificial and inferior (6)
4 Sunglasses (informal) (6)
8 Subject set for discussion (5)
9 Prolonged artillery fire (7)
10 Widow Twankey's principal boy (7)
11 Execute mob-handed without trial (5)
12 Competitor about whose abilities little is known (4,5)
17 Spanish appetisers (5)
19 Act of imputing blame or guilt (7)
21 Most northerly town in the British Isles (7)
22 Inhumanly cruel person (5)
23 Savour — sauce (6)
24 Ice over (6)

DOWN

1 Bit players (6)
2 Attendant — wed star (anag) (7)
3 Have a prevailing direction (5)
5 Horse that races 'over the sticks' (7)
6 Bleed (5)
7 Smoulder (6)
9 Criterion (9)
13 Yokels (7)
14 Trap (7)
15 Alters (anag) — less fresh (6)
16 Carefree and happy (6)
18 Exposure to harm (5)
20 Highland Games event (5)

Solution see page 253

83

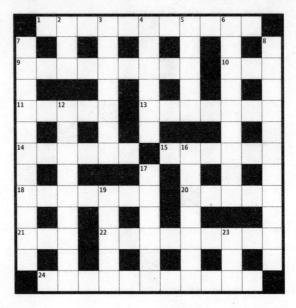

ACROSS

1 Stimulator of desire (11)
9 Furry Oz native (5,4)
10 Snow slider (3)
11 Start (5)
13 Sentimental (7)
14 Send abroad (6)
15 Again (6)
18 Herbaceous perennial flowering plant — air fees (anag) (7)
20 Descriptive of restricted residential community (5)
21 Bath, say (3)
22 Great artist of former times (3,6)
24 Medieval performance on a biblical theme (7,4)

DOWN

2 Edible seed (3)
3 Oven-ready bird (7)
4 Lackadaisical (6)
5 Pointy-nosed, mouse-like animal (5)
6 Not drinking (9)
7 Annual Munich event, centred on beer (11)
8 Spread unconfirmed scandal (4,3,4)
12 Domination (9)
16 Light used in murky conditions (3,4)
17 Male goose (6)
19 Inhale recreational drug through the nose (5)
23 Drink from China? (3)

Solution see page 253

84

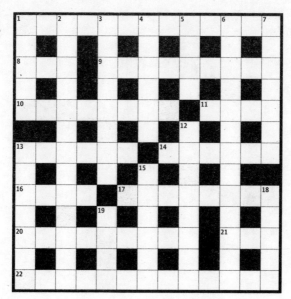

ACROSS

1 Deadpan (8-5)
8 Little devil (3)
9 Plant of the primrose family — limper pen (anag) (9)
10 Capsize (4,4)
11 Dark blue (4)
13 Two-digit prime (6)
14 Took it easy (6)
16 Gaelic language (4)
17 Files containing information (8)
20 Confused situation (9)
21 Old French coin (3)
22 Trashy — shoddy (5,3,5)

DOWN

1 Adhere (5)
2 Blameworthy (13)
3 Made better (8)
4 Tool (used with a sickle?) (6)
5 Charges for professional services (4)
6 Alternative to spectacles (7,6)
7 Held up (7)
12 Small measure used in recipes — open oats (anag) (8)
13 Wistfully mournful (7)
15 Grotesque sprite (6)
18 Read carefully (5)
19 Putsch (4)

Solution see page 253

85

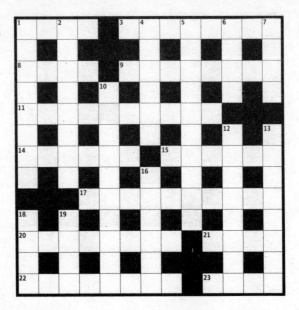

ACROSS

1 Outdoor pool (4)

3 Total traffic jam (8)

8 Unit of electrical potential (4)

9 Cosmetic surgery to remove signs of aging (8)

11 Rich man with a much younger girlfriend (5,5)

14 Item of party food (6)

15 Vegetation-destroying grasshopper (6)

17 Striking (10)

20 Thick-ribbed trouser fabric (8)

21 Old sailors' tipple (4)

22 Orwellian language (8)

23 Cut a design into (4)

DOWN

1 Nauseatingly infatuated? (8)

2 Assiduous (8)

4 40th US president, d. 2004 (6)

5 Rastafarian hairstyle (10)

6 Short biography of someone who has died (abbr) (4)

7 Friends (4)

10 Three-step event (6,4)

12 Eruption (8)

13 Might (8)

16 Hindu or Buddhist temple (6)

18 Examine intensely — examine superficially (4)

19 Black bird (4)

Solution see page 254

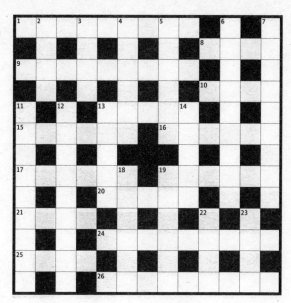

ACROSS

1 Please wait a second! (3,6)
8 Disgusting (4)
9 Negative vote to veto (9)
10 Stupid person (4)
13 The King (5)
15 Three times as many (6)
16 Protein produced by cells that acts as a biochemical catalyst (6)
17 Person who fails to cancel — who's on (anag) (2–4)
19 Group of performers (6)
20 Fresh (5)
21 Accepted standard of behaviour (4)
24 Left — dissolute (9)
25 Rich soil of sand and clay (4)
26 Shallow bowl used to culture bacteria — priest hid (anag) (5,4)

DOWN

2 Having the value zero — void (4)
3 Filth (4)
4 Telephone (6)
5 See 6
6,5 On no account (3,2,4,6)
7 Squashed (9)
11 Obliquely (2,2,5)
12 Counterpane (9)
13 First name of singer/songwriter born Reginald Dwight in 1947 (5)
14 Tangle (5)
18 Sway unsteadily (6)
19 Bank note (6)
22 Grip (4)
23 Large edible mushrooms (4)

Solution see page 254

87

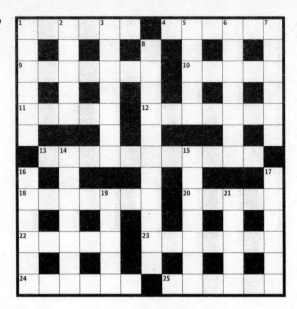

ACROSS

1 Long pieces of tartan worn over the shoulder (6)

4 Sphere-shaped (6)

9 Motley assortment (7)

10 One critical of the motives of others (5)

11 Light amplification by stimulated emission of radiation (5)

12 Position carrying full responsibility (3,4)

13 Wanton (11)

18 Rejection (7)

20 Consumed (5)

22 Crafty behaviour (5)

23 (Of a project) cause to sink without trace (7)

24 Informal collarless top (1–5)

25 Hard blow with a flat object (6)

DOWN

1 Stuff and nonsense (6)

2 Extensive landed property (often rolling) (5)

3 Line drawing (7)

5 Lawful (5)

6 Narrow piece of ribbon worn round the head (7)

7 Discover the position of something (6)

8 Sink to the floor with legs apart (2,3,6)

14 Dashing (7)

15 Discover (7)

16 Vivid (6)

17 Open (a bottle) (6)

19 Direct (a bullock?) (5)

21 Eighth letter in the Greek alphabet (5)

Solution see page 254

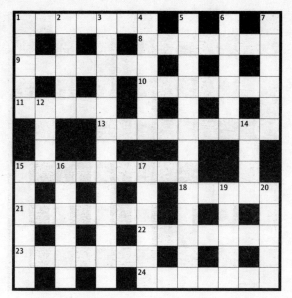

88

ACROSS

1 Charged with an offence (7)
8 Sexually explicit art (7)
9 Port near the mouth of the Elbe (7)
10 Gets back (7)
11 Chide (5)
13 So (9)
15 Dad's Army actor, d. 2012 (5,4)
18 Arrogant (5)
21 Thick scarf (7)
22 Perpetual (7)
23 Entrails (7)
24 Cash receipts (7)

DOWN

1 One of the Three Musketeers (5)
2 Brooch with an engraving in low relief (5)
3 Notify others of an emergency (5,3,5)
4 Gradation on a scale (6)
5 Ironic (6-2-5)
6 Japanese martial art (6)
7 Young Scottish girl (6)
12 Fossil fuel (4)
14 Loose rugby scrum (4)
15 Entered (4,2)
16 Young child (6)
17 Discontent verging on insurrection (6)
19 Cathedral cleric (5)
20 Shouts (5)

Solution see page 254

89

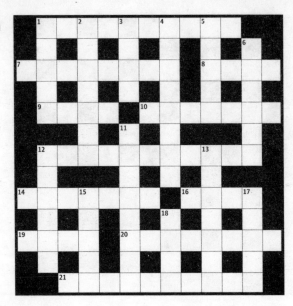

ACROSS

1 Signal letter Q, flown to indicate ship is carrying disease (6,4)

7 Marsupial that boxes (8)

8 Ukrainian capital (4)

9 System of weights for measuring precious metals and gemstones (4)

10 Entertainment industry (7)

12 Hot and cold sweet (5,6)

14 Lethargy (7)

16 Truncheon (4)

19 Slovenly layabout (4)

20 Youngster (8)

21 Varied collection (10)

DOWN

1 Leavening agent (5)

2 Long and tedious effort involved in gathering basic information (7)

3 Gumbo (4)

4 Small area captured and held as the basis for subsequent advance (8)

5 Crooked (5)

6 Eye part (6)

11 Sea between Italy and the Balkans (8)

12 Mess up (6)

13 Dried pale yellow seedless grape (7)

15 Jewish teacher (5)

17 Athletic and muscular (nonvegetarian?) (5)

18 Longitudinal structure supporting the frame of a vessel (4)

Solution see page 255

90

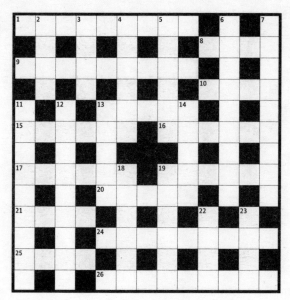

ACROSS

1 Maritime disaster (9)
8 Seaside structure (4)
9 Entrance hall (9)
10 Instruction to stop (4)
13 Film (5)
15 Servile follower (6)
16 Soft drink (6)
17 Excessive (French) (2,4)
19 Highly seasoned sausage (6)
20 Heartless (5)
21 Given the chop (4)
24 Design or guide for making something (9)
25 Completely ended (4)
26 Skill in a particular field (9)

DOWN

2 Hastened (4)
3 Cooking utensils (4)
4 Walter Scott novel (3,3)
5 French channel port (6)
6 Immediately (5,4)
7 Inhale (7,2)
11 Colosseum combatant (9)
12 Strewn (9))
13 Red wine from an area of southwest France (5)
14 Peer (5)
18 Verbose (6)
19 Rigorous — harsh (6)
22 Horse's gait (4)
23 Burden — responsibility (4)

Solution see page 255

91

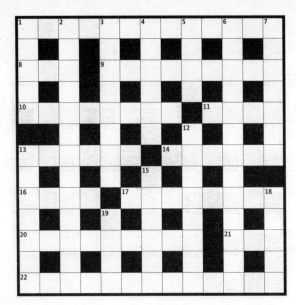

ACROSS

1 Inaccurate (4,2,3,4)

8 Numbers (abbr) (3)

9 Highland game bird — giant ramp (anag) (9)

10 One suffering memory loss (8)

11 Islamic ruler (4)

13 Responds (6)

14 Aniseed–flavoured aperitif (6)

16 Welsh industrialist and social reformer, founder of cooperative communities, d. 1858 (4)

17 African capital on the Congo River (8)

20 From another point of view (4,5)

21 Scottish John (3)

22 Naval NCOs (5,8)

DOWN

1 Money (informal) (5)

2 Withdrawal (13)

3 Facing (8)

4 Without exception (2,1,3)

5 Austen novel (4)

6 Quarrelsome (13)

7 Closely related (7)

12 European capital, venue for the 1952 Olympics (8)

13 Building's highest point (7)

15 Rice dish (6)

18 Female relatives (5)

19 Ill–defined (4)

Solution see page 255

92

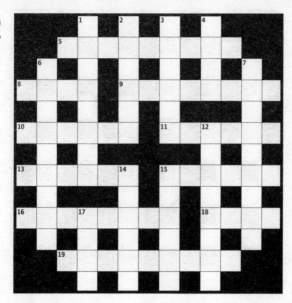

ACROSS

5 Greek dramatist, author of Oedipus Rex (9)

8 Metal, Au (4)

9 Tire oneself out (6,2)

10 Mad (6)

11 Flat-topped pieces of furniture (which can be turned?) (6)

13 Sand trap (6)

15 US state, capital Salem (6)

16 Suffered anguish (8)

18 Food fish related to the cod (4)

19 Stolen (9)

DOWN

1 Refrain — restrain — retain (4,4)

2 Protective finish on motor vehicle fittings (6)

3 Take — consent (6)

4 Flex (4)

6 Lunar rover (4,5)

7 Pyrotechnics (9)

12 President of the USSR, 1977–82 (8)

14 Consequence (6)

15 South London theatre (3,3)

17 Substantive (4)

Solution see page 255

93

ACROSS

1 Not so difficult (6)
4 Single figure (5)
7 Environment (6)
8 Rodent-catching cat (6)
9 Vivacity (4)
10 Made ready (8)
12 Work of outstanding artistry (11)
17 Obvious — clumsy (8)
19 Renown (4)
20 Gaffes (6)
21 Engrave (6)
22 Grass-like plant growing in wet places (5)
23 Stick one's oar in (6)

DOWN

1 Witty saying (7)
2 Mariners (7)
3 Kit (9)
4 Hang down loosely (5)
5 Pertaining to the stomach (7)
6 Diatribe (6)
11 Swear word (9)
13 Guaranteed (7)
14 Obliterated (7)
15 As a group (2,5)
16 New York borough (6)
18 Endured (5)

Solution see page 256

94

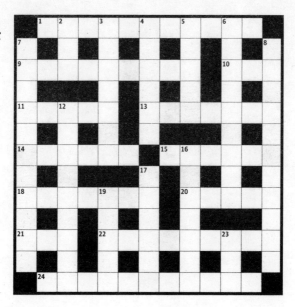

ACROSS

1 Now (2,3,6)

9 Risky ventures (4,5)

10 Compete (for) (3)

11 Rubbed clean (5)

13 Hormone that regulates the storage of glycogen in the liver (7)

14 Illicitly distilled liquor (6)

15 Legal proceeding brought by one party against another (6)

18 Farewell (7)

20 Herb of the mint family (5)

21 Slightly dotty (3)

22 Those allowed to sell alcoholic drinks (9)

24 Damage of anything sacred (11)

DOWN

2 X (3)

3 Of a strictly orthodox Jewish sect (7)

4 Member of the Unification Church (6)

5 Contemplates (5)

6 Small gimmicky knick-knacks (9)

7 Reveal a secret (4,3,4)

8 Having no significance (11)

12 Preliminary version from which other forms may be developed (9)

16 Piece of furniture with doors, shelves and drawers (7)

17 Swordsman (6)

19 Contradict (5)

23 One's self-image (3)

Solution see page 256

95

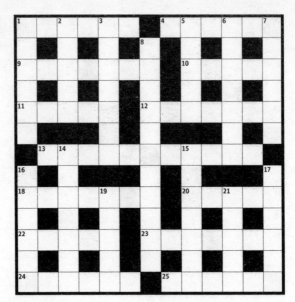

ACROSS

1 Hoity-toity (2-2-2)

4 Organised persecution of an ethnic group (6)

9 Strong feeling (7)

10 Presbyter (5)

11 Done (5)

12 Bring into servitude (7)

13 Dealer in small items used in sewing (11)

18 One barracking a public speaker (7)

20 Coarse plant food, low in nutrients (5)

22 Court card (5)

23 Bed of sedimentary rock (7)

24 Negligent (6)

25 Concealed (6)

DOWN

1 Circuited (6)

2 Medicated (5)

3 Grow less — waste away (7)

5 Does what one is told (5)

6 Excessive bureaucracy (3,4)

7 Homicide (very noisy when blue) (6)

8 Subject to improper coercion (5,6)

14 Enthusiastic and public praise (7)

15 Flavouring derived from a species of crocus (7)

16 Close-fitting necklace (6)

17 Moralising lecture (6)

19 Welsh vegetables? (5)

21 Go swimming (5)

Solution see page 256

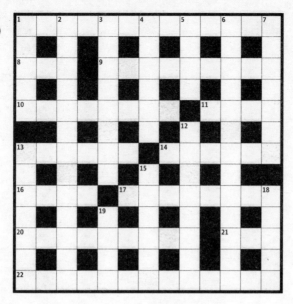

ACROSS

1 Before you can say Jack Robinson (5,2,1,5)

8 Muhammad ___ (or MacGraw?) (3)

9 Pitch in (4,1,4)

10 Naughtiness (8)

11 The Buckeye State (4)

13 Organic fertiliser (6)

14 Runcible eating irons? (6)

16 Average — standard (4)

17 Angels (8)

20 Yowl (9)

21 Exclude (3)

22 Take very great risks (4,4,5)

DOWN

1 Misgiving (5)

2 Quirky (13)

3 Desert of south-west Africa (8)

4 Abrasive tool (6)

5 Apartment (4)

6 Morbid fear of spiders (13)

7 Ugly (7)

12 Aghast (8)

13 Threatened (7)

15 Formally reject a former belief (6)

18 Undergo transformation (5)

19 Become bigger (4)

Solution see page 256

ACROSS

1 Large hard sweet (10)

7 Yield (7)

8 Mocking exclamation of laughter (2-3)

10 __ Novello, Welsh composer and songwriter, d. 1951 (4)

11 Bedspread (8)

13 Easily offended (6)

15 Incombustible matter left in the fireplace (6)

17 Hypothetical (8)

18 Pedestrian shopping area (4)

21 Down on a map (5)

22 Rotary engine (7)

23 Discarded (6,4)

DOWN

1 Nocturnal lizard (5)

2 Depressed (4)

3 Also (2,4)

4 Pitiful (8)

5 Breathed out (7)

6 Helpers (10)

9 Spellbound (10)

12 Chattanooga train? (4-4)

14 Falsehood (7)

16 First English printer, d.1491/2 (6)

19 Friendship (5)

20 Native American — bird (4)

Solution see page 257

98

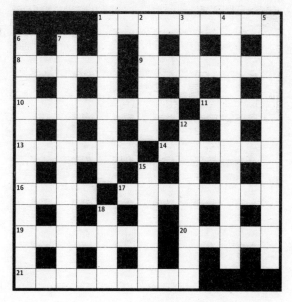

ACROSS

1 Not more than (2,3,4)
8 Comes into contact with (5)
9 Large aquatic mammal — sea cow (7)
10 Pleasure-seeker (8)
11 Platform (4)
13 Have a craving for (6)
14 The scenic route? (6)
16 Injure, causing permanent disability (4)
17 Carried out completely and carefully (8)
19 Raise petty objections (7)
20 Rhone (anag) — bird (5)
21 Process of becoming smaller (9)

DOWN

1 Pyromaniac (8)
2 Most domesticated (6)
3 Sicilian volcano (4)
4 Surpass by superior strategy (12)
5 Game where players try to find things by following a series of clues (8,4)
6 Speed is one of them (12)
7 Sign of bastardy on a coat of arms (4,8)
12 I haven't a clue (6,2)
15 Period of play in a polo match (6)
18 Dignified manner (4)

Solution see page 257

99

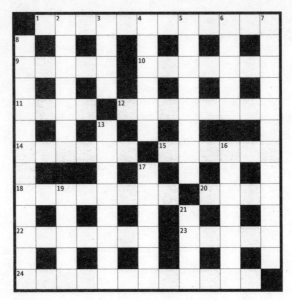

ACROSS

1 Instruction on a hotel bedroom door? (2,3,7)

9 With toad-like blemishes (5)

10 Guidance (7)

11 Academy of Television Arts and Sciences award (4)

12 Current beneath breaking wave (8)

14 Malicious — licentious (6)

15 Fleshy bit of the buttocks (6)

18 Place of trials (3,5)

20 Thrash (4)

22 Woolly (7)

23 Online message (5)

24 Of a large city — London Underground line (12)

DOWN

2 Rower (7)

3 Long-horned African antelope (4)

4 Pour wine into another container (6)

5 Pot (8)

6 Unexpected result (5)

7 Unfair (5,3,4)

8 Garden pink — Willie wet Sam (anag) (5,7)

13 US state (with a beetle) (8)

16 Ultimate tranquil state (7)

17 Pretty cave (6)

19 Cereal grass (5)

21 Food shop (abbr) (4)

Solution see page 257

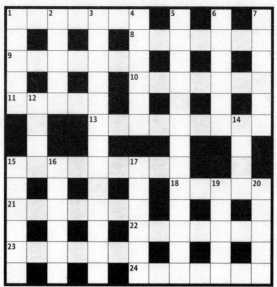

ACROSS

1 Flower (7)
8 Expressing love (7)
9 One who speaks excessively (7)
10 Nasal aperture (7)
11 Sloping mass of loose rock (5)
13 Rest (9)
15 Intermediary (2–7)
18 Trials — tribulations (5)
21 Offensive remarks (7)
22 Shopping container (7)
23 (Of pasta) firm when eaten (2,5)
24 Slices of bacon (7)

DOWN

1 Game on a green (5)
2 Proprietor (5)
3 Aggressive display of military force (5–8)
4 Large bottle (6)
5 Painstaking (13)
6 Very unpleasant (6)
7 Old stableman at an inn — sterol (anag) (6)
12 Small north Pacific salmon (4)
14 Compass point (4)
15 Six-stringed instrument (6)
16 Compared with (6)
17 Festival after Lent (6)
19 Balm — ointment (5)
20 Eye infections (5)

Solution see page 257

101

ACROSS

1 Confronted the unpleasant consequences of one's actions (5,3,5)

8 Recover from illness (3,4)

9 Push gently against (5)

10 Bloke (4)

11 Musical instrument — lime curd (anag) (8)

13 Cosmetics for self-beautification (4-2)

14 Reduce in status (6)

17 Strongly fortified defensive place (8)

19 Fingerprints (slang) (4)

21 A single shot (5)

22 Favouring force rather than diplomacy (7)

24 Captured (5,8)

DOWN

1 Bafflement (3)

2 Reduction in expenditure (7)

3 Eat sparingly (4)

4 Inert gas (6)

5 Shackles (8)

6 Gomorrah's partner in evil by the Dead Sea (5)

7 Gloomy — depressing (9)

10 Win (4,5)

12 Went to bed (6,2)

15 Formal speech (7)

16 __ Rantzen, TV presenter, b. 1940 (6)

18 Smelled disgusting (5)

20 Slow (anag) — bird of prey (4)

23 That woman (3)

Solution see page 258

102

ACROSS

1 Popular starter (5,8)
8 Low wall along a roof edge (7)
9 Lowest point (5)
10 Noise of a small object dropping into water (4)
11 Old campaigner (8)
13 Nervously restrained laugh (6)
14 Hitchcock's 1960 classic (6)
17 Event (8)
19 Expression of grief (4)
21 Large flow of liquid (5)
22 Those leaving their own country for political reasons (7)
24 Pell-mell (6–7)

DOWN

1 Get-up-and-go (3)
2 Par trio (anag) — Charles de Gaulle, say (7)
3 Small bites (4)
4 Robin Hood figure? (6)
5 Capital of the Democratic Republic of the Congo (8)
6 Birch relative (5)
7 Relating to theft (9)
10 Abraham or Isaac, perhaps (9)
12 French cop (8)
15 Guilty party (7)
16 Except if (6)
18 Not rude (5)
20 Gripper — fault (4)
23 Title for a baronet (3)

Solution see page 258

103

ACROSS

1 Agreement ending a dispute (10)

7 Type of lettuce (7)

8 Drinking chocolate (5)

10 Piece of legislation — one of the Clintons (4)

11 Quadruple (8)

13 Too (6)

15 Emphasis (6)

17 Public open space in Central London (4,4)

18 Attempt (4)

21 Less often seen (5)

22 Old saw (7)

23 Almost without hope (10)

DOWN

1 Period of time (5)

2 Ash, for example (4)

3 Body of salt water cut off from the sea (6)

4 Cream tea (anag) — soften by steeping in liquid (8)

5 Congratulatory phrase (4,3)

6 1984's totalitarian controller — TV reality show (3,7)

9 African capital (5,5)

12 Balderdash (8)

14 Back (7)

16 Visit informally (4,2)

19 Short online message (5)

20 One of Hamlet's questionable options? (2,2)

Solution see page 258

104

ACROSS

1 Ridge of sand (4)

3 Cultivated plant of the genus Delphinium (8)

9 Redwood (7)

10 Braid (5)

11 Enclose snugly (5)

12 Chinwag (6)

14 Eloquent and plausible (6–7)

17 Fabric stiffener (6)

19 1941 film about a young circus elephant born with large ears (5)

22 Lloyd Webber musical (5)

23 Omitted (4,3)

24 Native American axe (8)

25 Ever so (4)

DOWN

1 Scatter (8)

2 Muslim women's veil (5)

4 Illegal (7,3,3)

5 Completely broken down (5)

6 Area of high level ground (7)

7 Relative speed (of progress) (4)

8 Caress (6)

13 Idolatry (anag) — with skill (8)

15 Lightest metallic element (7)

16 Fall asleep (3,3)

18 Freshwater fish (5)

20 Bond actor, Roger, d. 2017 (5)

21 First in line (4)

Solution see page 258

105

ACROSS

1 Checker of accounts (7)

8 Corsican capital (7)

9 Perils (7)

10 Type of cigar (7)

11 Keep out (5)

13 Obtained dishonestly (3–6)

15 Photographers who pursue celebrities (9)

18 Annoyed (5)

21 Device for producing a tan (7)

22 Capacious bag (7)

23 Vivid written or oral descriptions (7)

24 Traditional name for a fox (7)

DOWN

1 Extra (5)

2 Star in Cygnus (5)

3 Personification of death (3,4,6)

4 Scamp (6)

5 Flatly (13)

6 Address aggressively (6)

7 Liquefied by heat (6)

12 Old Testament book and rabbi (4)

14 Greek equivalent of Cupid (4)

15 Female organ of a flower (6)

16 American friend via correspondence (6)

17 Gentle breeze (6)

19 US 1944 D–Day landing beach (5)

20 Substantial (5)

Solution see page 259

106

ACROSS

1 Incorporating all the newest ideas and features (5,2,3,3)

8 Air pollution (4)

9 Convert from code into plain language (8)

10 District of Paris, associated with many artists (10)

12 Dessert (6)

14 Delicate and pale in colour (6)

15 (Product) for removing unwanted hair (10)

19 Culinary herb (8)

20 Water-filled defensive trench (4)

21 Rodent kept as a pet (6,7)

DOWN

2 Author of The Bonfire of the Vanities (3,5)

3 Inebriated (5)

4 Trying experiences (7)

5 Implied — inferred (5)

6 Articulate (7)

7 Tall woody grass (4)

11 Diminish (8)

13 Borne (7)

14 Cornmeal — on plate (anag) (7)

16 Heathen (5)

17 Weighty books (5)

18 Luminous sign of saintliness (4)

Solution see page 259

107

ACROSS

1 Composed of viscous liquid drops (6)

4 Container for writing fluid (6)

9 Exhaust physically and/or emotionally (7)

10 Light-headed — bewildered (5)

11 Irish police officer (5)

12 Swamp (7)

13 Trans-Siberian Railway terminus (11)

18 Hissy fit (7)

20 Spokes (5)

22 Glass pane securer (5)

23 Phase of Earth's satellite (3,4)

24 Write back (6)

25 Arranged in a ring structure (6)

DOWN

1 Makes less clear (6)

2 Broadcasting (2,3)

3 Large hawk-like bird of prey (7)

5 Elbow (5)

6 Spanish conquistador who conquered the Incas, d. 1541 (7)

7 Vexatious (6)

8 Transfer of power to a lower level (11)

14 Syrup that may see a cough off (7)

15 Very thin (7)

16 Imagined state of perfection (6)

17 With electromechanical body parts (6)

19 (Of words) sound the same (5)

21 Spill saliva (5)

Solution see page 259

108

ACROSS

1 Children's game (5,4,4)
8 And others (2,2)
9 Valise (8)
10 Looking shabby (4,2,4)
12 (In relation to a ship) behind (6)
14 Eastern temple (6)
15 Not based on reliable evidence (3-7)
19 Thick, hard shell (8)
20 Silver-tongued (4)
21 In the present circumstances (2,6,5)

DOWN

2 Free from restraint (3,5)
3 Man-made fibre (5)
4 Soldier's little rectangular metal cooking pot (4,3)
5 Lacking worldly experience (5)
6 Accumulation of uncompleted work (7)
7 Rapidly — dissipated (4)
11 Sticking (8)
13 Tombstone inscription (7)
14 Deal with in a routine way (7)
16 Memorise (5)
17 Darkness (5)
18 Jokes (4)

Solution see page 259

109

ACROSS

1 Laugh uncontrollably (4,5)
8 Discontinue — delivery (4)
9 Provided solace (9)
10 Distinctively sharp taste (4)
13 Assistants (5)
15 Conclusion (6)
16 Elephant in a song (6)
17 Old and dusty spider's trap (6)
19 Walking (2,4)
20 Elevate (5)
21 Simple board game, involving dice (4)
24 Contented (9)
25 The Mormon state (4)
26 Brass instruments (9)

DOWN

2 River flowing through Shakespeare's Stratford (4)
3 Elevator (4)
4 Golf score of one stroke under par (6)
5 Inconsistent in quality (6)
6 Type of carpet — a bold Moor (anag) (9)
7 Type of pasta (9)
11 Rather poorly (3,6)
12 Very poorly (2,1,3,3)
13 Change (5)
14 French river (5)
18 Charity sale of many different things (6)
19 Densest of all naturally occurring metallic elements, Os (6)
22 In that case … (2,2)
23 Lake — French mother (4)

Solution see page 260

110

ACROSS

1 Irish female spirit who warns of an impending death (7)
8 Dubious (7)
9 Passage selected from a book (7)
10 Composed wholly of top performers (3-4)
11 Pledge of fidelity (5)
13 Evermore (9)
15 Plebiscites (9)
18 Ancient seer — prophetess (5)
21 Bright ray — bus name (anag) (7)
22 Referee (7)
23 Fought, even to death (7)
24 Louis Armstrong's byname (7)

DOWN

1 French Atlantic naval base (5)
2 Tortilla chip served with savoury toppings (5)
3 Without compassion (4-9)
4 A group of buildings built together in one development (6)
5 With very bad eyesight (2,5,2,1,3)
6 Concerning teeth (6)
7 Firmly constructed (6)
12 Gardening tool (4)
14 Slothful (4)
15 Settle (6)
16 Digit (6)
17 Vagrant peoples (6)
19 Make a mess of (5)
20 (Musically) slow in tempo and broad in manner (5)

Solution see page 260

111

ACROSS

1 Join the opposing side in Parliament (5,3,5)
8 Lamentable (7)
9 Object surviving from the past (5)
10 Partly open (4)
11 Bullfighter (8)
13 Harsh order, allowing no discussion (6)
14 Coterie (6)
17 Eccentric (8)
19 Something owed (4)
21 More mature (5)
22 Chic — fashionable (7)
24 With an exaggerated sense of self-importance (7–6)

DOWN

1 Edible mushroom (3)
2 Remote and sparsely populated parts of Australia (7)
3 Easily yielding to pressure (4)
4 Wait a bit! (4,2)
5 Hitherto (8)
6 Eyed lecherously (5)
7 Occurring repeatedly (9)
10 Brazen (9)
12 Oily fish (8)
15 Expressed doubt about (7)
16 Deteriorate (6)
18 Electronic sound reproduction (5)
20 Funeral fire (4)
23 Concealed (3)

Solution see page 260

112

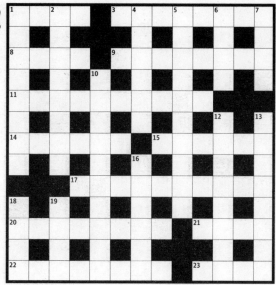

ACROSS

1 Pushing up daisies? (4)

3 Enquire about someone (3,5)

8 Mist coming in from the sea (4)

9 Right to act completely at one's own discretion (4,4)

11 There's no cause for alarm (3,2,5)

14 Fall back on (4,2)

15 Hasten (anag) — capital city (6)

17 Make an enemy of (10)

20 Cynical — so rancid (anag) (8)

21 Securely fixed (4)

22 Device for removing condensation from a windscreen (8)

23 Be inclined (to) (4)

DOWN

1 Clear-cut (8)

2 Opening (8)

4 Grief (6)

5 Deviation from the accepted norm (10)

6 Squad (4)

7 Go by horse (4)

10 Of great significance (10)

12 Ancestry (8)

13 Expressed agreement (8)

16 Deep, narrow gorge (6)

18 Manipulated (4)

19 Top edge of something (4)

Solution see page 260

113

ACROSS

1 One after another (13)
8 Highest point of achievement (4)
9 Treatment for the feet (8)
10 Commotion (10)
12 Get away (6)
14 Small yellow and black finch (6)
15 Somewhat (10)
19 Motherly (8)
20 Naked (4)
21 With a very tight budget (2,1,10)

DOWN

2 Naturally! (2,6)
3 Heave of the sea's surface (5)
4 Competent (7)
5 (Of the sea) ebbing and flowing (5)
6 Winners (7)
7 Traditional knowledge (4)
11 Co-founder of al-Qaida, killed 2011 (3,5)
13 Without purpose (7)
14 Excess (7)
16 No idea (informal) (5)
17 Carreras, for example (5)
18 Daybreak (4)

Solution see page 261

114

ACROSS

1 Written works of merit (10)
7 Case for holding a light (7)
8 Publication (5)
10 Eat (slang) — food (slang) (4)
11 Struggle clumsily (8)
13 Deep sleep-like state (6)
15 Knight of the Round Table — the rag (anag) (6)
17 Loaded with regret (8)
18 Uncritically admired object (4)
21 Quaintly amusing (5)
22 Contagious skin infection (7)
23 Parched (10)

DOWN

1 School punishment (5)
2 Rain cats and dogs (4)
3 Cause continuing irritation (6)
4 Court of arbitration (8)
5 What's left (7)
6 Mean-spirited (3-7)
9 Quality of being gross (10)
12 In fact (8)
14 One name (anag) — plant (7)
16 More intimate (6)
19 Wept (5)
20 Stop (4)

Solution see page 261

115

ACROSS

5 Military training exercise (9)
8 Fastener (4)
9 Diving apparatus (8)
10 Go back to a former practice (6)
11 Followed (6)
13 State of health (6)
15 Perplex (6)
16 Pimp (8)
18 Is in session (4)
19 Portrayal (9)

DOWN

1 Most spiteful (8)
2 Lauren Bacall's first actor husband, d. 1957 (6)
3 Majestic — month (6)
4 Viva (4)
6 Become disillusioned (4,5)
7 As a matter of fact (2,7)
12 Brew (8)
14 Eavesdrop (informal) (6)
15 Scold (6)
17 Masticate (4)

Solution see page 261

116

ACROSS

1 Medicated sweet (5,4)

8 Spirit in The Tempest (5)

9 Thick material with a raised pattern (7)

10 Three-hulled craft (8)

11 Flightless New Zealand bird (4)

13 Paid male escort (6)

14 Breakwater (6)

16 Way for pedestrians (4)

17 Musical note equal to half a minim (8)

19 For the time being (7)

20 Right-hand page of an open book (5)

21 Korean martial art (3,4,2)

DOWN

1 Guilty (8)

2 Cheerful — optimistic (6)

3 Rigid circular band (4)

4 Reminder of the true state of affairs (7,5)

5 Special liking or preference (12)

6 Position affording a good view (7,5)

7 Motionless street entertainer (6,6)

12 Large choral work (8)

15 German port city and state (6)

18 Ship's company (4)

Solution see page 261

117

ACROSS

5 Tall silky-haired dog (6,5)
7 Male offspring (4)
8 Praiseworthy (8)
9 Acquire (7)
11 Demise (5)
13 Comical (5)
14 Pungent condiment (7)
16 Self-government in local matters (4,4)
17 Incandescence (4)
18 More than is needed (11)

DOWN

1 Poultry products (4)
2 Visitors (7)
3 Raise one's voice (5)
4 Capital on the Danube (8)
5 Non-metric system of weights (11)
6 True oilseed (anag) — harmful (11)
10 Undisguised disrespect (8)
12 With little or no sound (7)
15 Hasten (5)
17 Proceed (2,2)

Solution see page 262

118

ACROSS

1 Standing — speaking (2,4,4)
7 Money saved for the future (4,3)
8 First in order of importance (5)
10 Otherwise (4)
11 Instrument — litre can (anag) (8)
13 Purify (6)
15 Someone on work experience? (6)
17 Distinction — high ground (8)
18 Half-baked — fly-by-night mammals (4)
21 Teach — followers (5)
22 In question (2,5)
23 Determined to do something at all costs (4-4,2)

DOWN

1 Fertile patch in a desert (5)
2 Do what one is told (4)
3 Overwhelm (6)
4 Conspicuously outrageous (8)
5 Delete for ever (7)
6 Word or phrase expressing affection (10)
9 Greatly surprised (10)
12 Hellish (8)
14 Warship smaller than a destroyer (7)
16 Embarrassing predicament (informal) (6)
19 Pyromania (5)
20 A just detectable amount (4)

Solution see page 262

119

ACROSS

1 Lacking generosity (12)
9 Leaves (5)
10 Laugh disrespectfully (7)
11 Public disturbance (4)
12 Liquorice flavoured liqueur (8)
14 Media boss (6)
15 Slight prickling sensation (6)
18 Female sweetheart (4-4)
20 Small ball with a hole through the middle (4)
22 Magpie (7)
23 Dramatic artist (5)
24 Fashion leaders (12)

DOWN

2 East African capital (7)
3 Party-giver (4)
4 Feel aggrieved at (6)
5 Alpinist (anag) — state of panic (8)
6 Give rise to (5)
7 Protection from loud noise (3,9)
8 Be informed of something (4,4,4)
13 Conspired together (8)
16 More renowned (7)
17 Strongly opposed (6)
19 Male bird (5)
21 Male deer (4)

Solution see page 262

120

ACROSS

1 Simultaneously (2,3,4,4)
8 An arm and a leg? (4)
9 Sardinian capital (8)
10 Fashionable (3,3,4)
12 Main course (6)
14 Hothead (6)
15 Share out (10)
19 Lack of any false pride (8)
20 Ornamental fabric (4)
21 Find ways of getting round regulations (4,3,6)

DOWN

2 Of little importance (8)
3 Addiction to a drug (5)
4 Small northern Pacific salmon (7)
5 Hot molten rock (5)
6 Hindmost part (4,3)
7 Extra (4)
11 Tiny amount (8)
13 Fit of extreme anger (3,4)
14 Persons suffering for their beliefs (7)
16 Worker in metals (5)
17 Invoices (5)
18 Regular hexahedron (4)

Solution see page 262

121

ACROSS

1 Drawn to (9)
8 Male pig (4)
9 Feeling of appreciation (9)
10 Horned animal (4)
13 Enchant (5)
15 Graceful (6)
16 Good long look (6)
17 Sprawl (6)
19 Burning with emotion (6)
20 Punctuation mark (5)
21 Begin to melt (4)
24 Part of the Mediterranean between Greece and Turkey (6,3)
25 Spirited — suggestive (4)
26 Authorised by law (9)

DOWN

2 Horse racing, generally (4)
3 Compassion — girl's name (4)
4 (Of a tune) instantly appealing and memorable (6)
5 Tolerate (6)
6 Ashamed (9)
7 Thrift (9)
11 3-D art form (9)
12 Vehicle designed to carry the sick (9)
13 Wooden-soled shoes (5)
14 Fragrant resin burned as incense (5)
18 First in order of birth (6)
19 Agreement (6)
22 Group that's part of a larger organisation (4)
23 Scoff (4)

Solution see page 263

122

ACROSS

1 Horrified (6)
4 Less in number (5)
7 Fruit (6)
8 Stimulus (6)
9 Young elephant (4)
10 Object of abhorrence (8)
12 Young hooligans (11)
17 One present at an event (8)
19 Spanish painter, d. 1828 (4)
20 Insubstantial (6)
21 County town of Devon (6)
22 Snag (5)
23 Social position — prestige (6)

DOWN

1 Give an ovation (7)
2 Co-operative (7)
3 Long drawn-out (9)
4 Deceptive manoeuvre (5)
5 Most crafty (7)
6 Annul an act of parliament (6)
11 Light-hearted pastime (9)
13 Uproot by force (7)
14 Treat carelessly (7)
15 Diffidence (7)
16 Affection (6)
18 Cardinal point (5)

Solution see page 263

123

ACROSS

1 Beast of burden (9)

8 Rejoice (5)

9 Shortfall (7)

10 More than anything else (5,3)

11 Tranquil (4)

13 French regional dialect (6)

14 Wanton destroyer (6)

16 Large number — killed (4)

17 Agnostic (anag) — moving easily (8)

19 Country on the Red Sea (7)

20 Chess pieces (5)

21 Spend money freely (6,3)

DOWN

1 Hopelessly inadequate (8)

2 Pamper — cook in nearly boiling water (6)

3 Fit of irritation (4)

4 US vice president, 1953–61 and president, 1969–74 (7,5)

5 One who studies insects (12)

6 Cyclists — women's calf-length trousers (5,7)

7 Mediocre (3-2-3-4)

12 Ancient official language of India (8)

15 Spud (6)

18 Greek god of war (4)

Solution see page 263

124

ACROSS

1 Granules used to make a yellow sauce (7,6)
8 Sparkle (7)
9 Of sound (5)
10 Clamp down teeth (4)
11 Short school break (4-4)
13 Very tired (6)
14 Very strict (6)
17 Steep descent (8)
19 Narrow strip of land almost surrounded by water (4)
21 Unable to move (5)
22 Pepys, for example (7)
24 Granules used to make a yellow paste (7,6)

DOWN

1 Toothed wheel (3)
2 Affected by something overwhelming (7)
3 Initial contribution to the common pot (4)
4 Cathedral city of north-east England (6)
5 Made rigid and set into a conventional pattern (8)
6 Needs (anag) — thick (5)
7 Lying down (9)
10 Ancient city on the Sea of Marmara (9)
12 Long bitter row (8)
15 Removed contents (7)
16 Dodged (6)
18 John Buchan used 39 of them (5)
20 Circle of light around the moon (4)
23 Sticky black stuff (3)

Solution see page 263

125

ACROSS

1 Florida's largest city and port — lock javelins (anag) (12)
9 So far (2,3)
10 Is an indication of (7)
11 American TV award (4)
12 Medium-sized chilli pepper (8)
14 Air (6)
15 Tolkien's small, hairy-footed person (6)
18 Recent arrival (8)
20 Dark purple (4)
22 Tosh (7)
23 Well! (2,3)
24 US nick (12)

DOWN

2 Very, very bad (7)
3 Friends and acquaintances (4)
4 Father — boss (3,3)
5 Hot curry (8)
6 Flexible (5)
7 Nice to look at (4,2,3,3)
8 Winning by dubious tactics (12)
13 Liqueur made with eggs, sugar and brandy (8)
16 Subcutaneous fat (7)
17 One with a mate who struts his stuff? (6)
19 On it, you're dry! (5)
21 Master of a Hindu spiritual and ascetic discipline (4)

Solution see page 264

126

ACROSS

5 Monkey business (11)
7 Eagerly desirous (4)
8 Abhorred (8)
9 Tallest land animal (7)
11 Dim — swoon (5)
13 Volunteer — proposal (5)
14 Riders in a race (7)
16 Lack of solidarity (8)
17 Cows' sounds (4)
18 Amused (11)

DOWN

1 Main news story (4)
2 Welsh capital (7)
3 Girl's name — pooled money (5)
4 Large mound of dried grass (8)
5 Social know-how (6,5)
6 Demon barber of Fleet Street (7,4)
10 Sufficient (8)
12 Imaginary monster, frightening to children (7)
15 Metric unit of capacity (5)
17 Numerous (4)

Solution see page 264

127

ACROSS

1 Pet bird (abbr) (6)
4 Butch (5)
7 Memorable saying (6)
8 Grow (6)
9 Second Greek letter (4)
10 Game played with netted sticks (8)
12 Astonish (11)
17 South African horn, seen at football matches (8)
19 Quacker? (4)
20 Excite — activate (4,2)
21 Scandinavian (6)
22 Short-tempered (5)
23 Move with a circular motion (6)

DOWN

1 Dried product of a laurel tree, used in cooking (3,4)
2 3-D model representing a scene (7)
3 Unable to be rubbed out (9)
4 Drink to combine with alcohol (5)
5 Structural framework of older cars (7)
6 A lot (6)
11 By all means (9)
13 Baby hare (7)
14 Principality in the Pyrenees (7)
15 Relating to touch (7)
16 Human or animal manifestation of Vishnu (6)
18 Polish currency unit (5)

Solution see page 264

128

ACROSS

1 Fabled one-eyed giant (7)
8 Body of troops arranged in a line (7)
9 Most humble (7)
10 Means of execution (3,4)
11 First premier of the Soviet Union, d. 1924 (5)
13 Based on personal accounts, possibly unreliable (9)
15 Stinks (9)
18 Praise (5)
21 Person from Barcelona? (7)
22 Young children's horses? (3–4)
23 Unintentional self-inflicted harm (3,4)
24 Give someone the right (7)

DOWN

1 Beast of burden (5)
2 Innocent (5)
3 Quite exceptional person (3,2,1,7)
4 Light upon (6)
5 Equestrian competition (5–3,5)
6 Very nearly (6)
7 Introduce publicly for the first time (6)
12 Per head (4)
14 Florence's river (4)
15 Slightly crazy — bird (6)
16 Still in existence (6)
17 Confused interwoven mass (6)
19 (Make a) chirping noise (5)
20 (Fabric woven with) a fine cotton thread (5)

Solution see page 264

129

ACROSS

1 Unlawful secret agreements (12)
9 Beaver's den (5)
10 Tension-filled (7)
11 Old (4)
12 Women's trousers, cut to resemble a skirt (8)
14 Ice cream with toppings (6)
15 One who has achieved a state of perfect enlightenment (6)
18 Hit man (5,3)
20 Mongolian tent (4)
22 Inflamed swelling (7)
23 Wastrel (5)
24 Inability to relax — lessen stress (anag) (12)

DOWN

2 My dear chap! (3,4)
3 Killed intentionally (4)
4 Inward flow (6)
5 Something seen as comparable to another (8)
6 Metal cast as a block (5)
7 Fulfilling expectations (12)
8 Defuses a tense situation by talking frankly (6,3,3)
13 Tactic of aggressive promotion (4,4)
16 Manx capital (7)
17 Invitees (6)
19 Supports (5)
21 Omen (4)

Solution see page 265

130

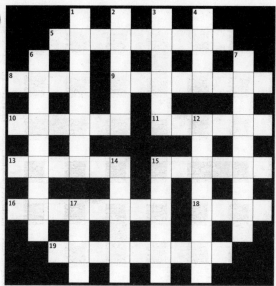

ACROSS

5 Deliberately harmful (9)
8 Work hard (4)
9 Death and decay of body tissue (8)
10 Floor level of a building (6)
11 Inferior — worthless (6)
13 Crowd (6)
15 Lying on one's back (6)
16 Reimbursement for goods damaged in transit (8)
18 Small insect-eating songbirds (4)
19 Unproductive (9)

DOWN

1 Australian animal — a no-go ark (anag) (8)
2 Small boat propelled with oars (6)
3 Small finch, once popular as a caged songbird (6)
4 Sound of a contented cat (4)
6 Arrow makers (9)
7 Without revealing who you are (9)
12 Jobs for the boys (8)
14 Without charge (6)
15 Malodorous (6)
17 Not functioning properly (4)

Solution see page 265

131

ACROSS

1 Flag — of the usual kind (8)
5 Competent (4)
9 Peers of the realm (5)
10 Vanity (7)
11 Soldiers regarded as expendable in battle (6,6)
13 Perplexed — rotten (6)
14 Exactly right (4,2)
17 Unbearable (12)
20 Beyond endurance (3,4)
21 Strident sound (5)
22 Established standards (4)
23 Marvellous (8)

DOWN

1 Lather (4)
2 Gauche — obstinate (7)
3 Not sincere (12)
4 Modern — centre (anag) (6)
6 Procreate (5)
7 Install as a 16 (8)
8 Ill-matched (12)
12 Imperial (8)
15 Manx parliament (7)
16 Chess piece (6)
18 Throng (5)
19 Tear apart (4)

Solution see page 265

132

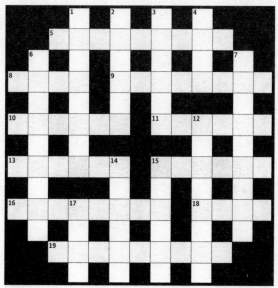

ACROSS

5 As partial payment with the rest to come later (2,7)

8 Distinctive area (4)

9 Energetic and unpredictable person (4,4)

10 Largest island of the Dodecanese (6)

11 Young middle-class professional with a luxurious life style (6)

13 Friends in Spain (6)

15 Talkative (6)

16 Sweet-smelling (8)

18 Front — confront (4)

19 Poke one's nose in (9)

DOWN

1 The one expected to lose (8)

2 Weighing machine (6)

3 Group of vehicles travelling together (6)

4 Wintry precipitation (4)

6 US second-year student (9)

7 Suspension of hostilities (9)

12 Supporting structure (8)

14 Remained (6)

15 Severed (3,3)

17 Firearms (4)

Solution see page 265

133

ACROSS

1 Instinctive response to a sudden threat (5,2,6)

8 Probabilities (4)

9 Dreadful (8)

10 Speed up (10)

12 Voters (anag) — made every effort (6)

14 Grave (6)

15 Incorrect (10)

19 Not in any way restrained (8)

20 Feeling in need of an aspirin? (4)

21 Christian Science movement founder (4,5,4)

DOWN

2 Show (8)

3 Possible cause of careless mistakes? (5)

4 Lewd (7)

5 __ MacDonald, heroine of the 1745 Jacobite rising (5)

6 Old school desk feature (7)

7 Attila's people (4)

11 Waylaid (8)

13 Not working (3,4)

14 Bind tight with clothes (7)

16 Sign of the scales (5)

17 Likeness (5)

18 Palindromic girl's name (4)

Solution see page 266

134

ACROSS

1 Flung (6)

4 Rules or regulations adopted by an organisation (6)

9 Brief and to the point (7)

10 Short surplice worn by Catholic priests — to act (anag) (5)

11 Stratospheric layer of gas — invigorating sea air (5)

12 Lured (7)

13 Timeless cob (anag) — food (11)

18 My house in France? (4,3)

20 Partial or comparative darkness (5)

22 Lubricated (5)

23 Soon (poetically) (7)

24 Group of seven performers (6)

25 Provide with garments (6)

DOWN

1 Browbeat (6)

2 Beatles drummer (5)

3 Look with the power to inflict harm (4,3)

5 Sailing vessel (5)

6 The — thing (7)

7 Beer and lemonade mixture (6)

8 Building site revolver? (6,5)

14 Coincide partly (7)

15 Samuel Johnson's biographer (7)

16 Horizontally (6)

17 Popular music of Jamaican origin (6)

19 Tiny fly (5)

21 Approximately (5)

Solution see page 266

135

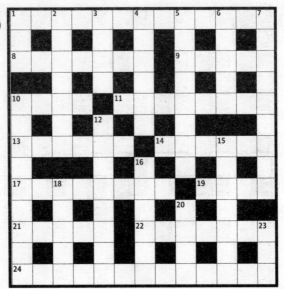

ACROSS

1 Policy of strict law enforcement (4,9)

8 Distressing (7)

9 Established (3,2)

10 Cry loudly (4)

11 Back to front (8)

13 Sri Lanka, formerly (6)

14 Means of avoiding something (3-3)

17 Retract (8)

19 Defended successfully (4)

21 Forbidden (5)

22 Haven (7)

24 Norwegian polar explorer d. 1928 (5,8)

DOWN

1 Fastener (3)

2 Romney, Hythe & Dymchurch, for example (7)

3 Petty quarrel (4)

4 Soothed (6)

5 Cockney tea (5,3)

6 Brief written records (5)

7 Speeded up (9)

10 Isolated spot (9)

12 West Sussex racecourse (8)

15 Taxing (7)

16 Come to understand (6)

18 Shin bone (5)

20 Broad smile (4)

23 Uninterrupted sequence (3)

Solution see page 266

136

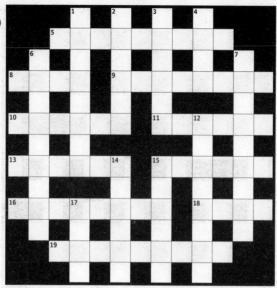

ACROSS

5 Smear (9)

8 Drone — bustle (4)

9 Specific design and size for printing letters, numbers and characters (8)

10 Friendly (6)

11 Swallow (6)

13 Up to speed (from French) (2,4)

15 Hallucination caused by hot air (6)

16 Sand-filled device traditionally used in the kitchen (3-5)

18 Average (2-2)

19 Verbatim (9)

DOWN

1 Kind of Italian restaurant (8)

2 Disorganised (6)

3 Scottish water sprite — Australian sheepdog (6)

4 Short repeated phrase in popular music or jazz (4)

6 Beach vehicle (4,5)

7 Student of living things and their environment (9)

12 In a cheap and flashy way (8)

14 'Tree falling!' (6)

15 Brick bonder (6)

17 Back end (4)

Solution see page 266

137

ACROSS

1 Menacing (8)

5 Secular (4)

9 Dromedary (5)

10 Ramshackle (2,5)

11 It keeps hair oil off the back of a chair (12)

13 Nabokov's nymphet (6)

14 Swiss house with sloping roof and wide eaves (6)

17 Went from bad to worse (12)

20 (Of time) passed (7)

21 Audibly (5)

22 Architect of Buckingham Palace, d. 1835 (4)

23 Car on end (anag) — artillery (8)

DOWN

1 Dissenting clique (4)

2 In name only (7)

3 Concern for number one (4-8)

4 Hebrew prophet who rebuked Ahab and Jezebel (6)

6 First sign of the zodiac (5)

7 Male singer operated on before puberty to retain his soprano voice (8)

8 Relax after a crisis (7,5)

12 Beat repeatedly with a heavy object (8)

15 Now idle (anag) — short rest (3-4)

16 Give thought to (6)

18 Golf course hazards (5)

19 Not in active use (4)

Solution see page 267

138

ACROSS

1 Take by surprise (5,8)
8 Rack by a sink for letting crockery dry (7)
9 Scruffs of the neck (5)
10 Bundle (of hay?) (4)
11 Lazy (4–4)
13 Cloth in which a body is wrapped for burial (6)
14 Decapitate (6)
17 Indirect reference (8)
19 Level (4)
21 Cut into cubes (5)
22 Form a mental picture (7)
24 Without compunction, pity, or compassion (13)

DOWN

1 Rotter (3)
2 Short film advertising a forthcoming feature (7)
3 Suspend (4)
4 Constricted (6)
5 Itinerant (8)
6 Waterway where the current runs very fast (5)
7 Strap to hold up a stocking (9)
10 Onlooker (9)
12 Someone not accepted by society (8)
15 Draws out (7)
16 Relating to cattle (6)
18 Temporary replacement doctor (5)
20 Sugar merchant and art gallery philanthropist, founder, d. 1899 (4)
23 Cathedral city in East Anglia (3)

Solution see page 267

139

ACROSS

1 Calculate (6)

4 Make less clear (5)

7 (Of a job) allocate to someone (6)

8 Large cave (6)

9 Stage area out of sight of the audience (4)

10 Failed to listen correctly (8)

12 Killing oneself (6,2,3)

17 Unquestioning supporter — aspirant (anag) (8)

19 Mines (4)

20 Impervious to sight (6)

21 Cleric — canoed (anag) (6)

22 Browned bread (5)

23 Card suit (6)

DOWN

1 Temporary relief (7)

2 Recoiled in fear (7)

3 Emollients (9)

4 Disagree violently (5)

5 Protective garment worn over ordinary clothes (7)

6 Clear so that nothing is left (6)

11 Swim naked (6-3)

13 Place of complete bliss (7)

14 Clap (7)

15 Liquid preparations for the skin (7)

16 Choose not to take part (3,3)

18 Indigenous Greenlanders (5)

Solution see page 267

140

ACROSS

1 Additional (13)
8 Signal fires (7)
9 Mountains on the boundary between Europe and Asia (5)
10 Transvestite's garb (4)
11 Disturb (8)
13 Underpants (6)
14 Means of acquiring a tan (6)
17 Lab vessel (4,4)
19 Stratagem (4)
21 Short (5)
22 Marine mammal (7)
24 Undemanding popular music (4,9)

DOWN

1 Weep convulsively (3)
2 Body of troops in close formation (7)
3 Get an eyeful (4)
4 Pondering (6)
5 Feeling about to vomit (8)
6 Separated (5)
7 The recent past (9)
10 Moot (9)
12 Showing appreciation (8)
15 Song from South Pacific (4,3)
16 Homes (6)
18 Places for pigs (5)
20 Do a runner (4)
23 Horse — badger (3)

Solution see page 267

141

ACROSS

1 Armed guard on a plane (3,7)

7 G in MGM (7)

8 One shunning animal products (5)

10 Decomposes (4)

11 Physical effort (8)

13 Unoccupied (6)

15 Phases (6)

17 Grotesque misrepresentation (8)

18 Long narrative poem (4)

21 First appearance (5)

22 Of Spain and Portugal (7)

23 Brains (4,6)

DOWN

1 Croatian port (5)

2 Two-masted sailing boat (4)

3 Extension to a building (6)

4 Harshness (8)

5 Pursuit with hook, line and sinker? (7)

6 Made worse (10)

9 A very short time (10)

12 Family tree (8)

14 Compartment (7)

16 Most feared barbarian invader of the Roman Empire, d. 453 (6)

19 Previous (5)

20 Metrical units (4)

Solution see page 268

142

ACROSS

1 Receive voluntarily (6)
4 Provide (6)
8 Snares (5)
9 Long narrow flag (7)
10 Tycoon (7)
11 Wide open (5)
12 Intrepid (9)
17 Picture puzzle (5)
19 Undertaken (7)
21 Large Spanish sailing ship (7)
22 Fix computer program problems (5)
23 Pamphlets (6)
24 Vipers (6)

DOWN

1 'Season of mists and mellow fruitfulness' (6)
2 Modified (7)
3 Tagliatelle, for example (5)
5 Short piece of music played on brass instruments (for the Common Man?) (7)
6 44th US president (5)
7 Responsibilities (6)
9 Welsh seaside resort — past entry (anag) (9)
13 Punnets (anag) — still available (7)
14 Capable of being solved (in water?) (7)
15 Orville or Wilbur? (6)
16 Maxims (6)
18 Wood used by model makers (5)
20 Given up (5)

Solution see page 268

143

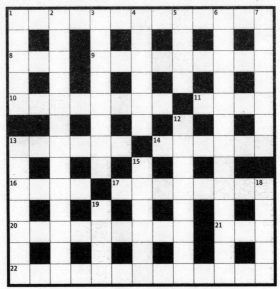

ACROSS

1 People are going to cop it (5,4,4)
8 Set on fire (3)
9 Amazing (9)
10 Hold dear (8)
11 Handled — material (4)
13 Wealthy and privileged person (3,3)
14 Licentious (6)
16 Staple food — English lyricist, b. 1944 (4)
17 Goodbye (8)
20 En route (2,7)
21 Behind (3)
22 Avoid committing oneself in a difficult situation (5,4,4)

DOWN

1 Serf in ancient Sparta (5)
2 Established as genuine (13)
3 What the Uxbridge and South Ruislip constituency is for Boris (4,4)
4 Pay no heed to (6)
5 Metal — Pb (4)
6 Working in harmony (2,3,4,4)
7 Settled — cold tea (anag) (7)
12 Sweet red peppers (8)
13 Fit out (7)
15 Small plum (6)
18 Sacred Egyptian water lily (5)
19 Valley (4)

Solution see page 268

144

ACROSS

1 Snide remarks (4)
3 Countrywide (8)
8 Equipment (4)
9 ___ Dali, painter (8)
11 Gondolier's song (10)
14 Sea cow — gun dog (anag) (6)
15 Senior nursing officer of old (6)
17 Small melon with ribbed skin (10)
20 Dirty (8)
21 Fine (for the Scots) (4)
22 Summer frock (8)
23 Wharf (4)

DOWN

1 One given menial tasks to do (8)
2 Best bib and tucker (4,4)
4 Female warrior (6)
5 Priceless (10)
6 Affirmative gestures (4)
7 Hang around in a secretive way (4)
10 Wagner opera (10)
12 (Sound made by) fancy frills on female dresses — four/four (anag) (4-4)
13 In motion (5,3)
16 Horses (6)
18 Worry unnecessarily (4)
19 Long-necked bird (4)

Solution see page 268

145

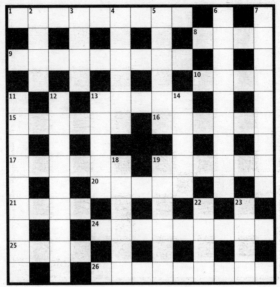

ACROSS

1 Central America country (5,4)
8 Be quiet! (4)
9 Start (9)
10 Metal (that may be pumped?) (4)
13 God of love (5)
15 Offensive remark (6)
16 Knife for stabbing (6)
17 Apparitions (6)
19 Inhuman (6)
20 Hirsute (5)
21 Wild cat with tufted ears (4)
24 Miss Italy? (9)
25 Undersea ridge (4)
26 Wesleyan (9)

DOWN

2 Comply with orders (4)
3 Castor or Pollux? (4)
4 Expire (3,3)
5 Frank (6)
6 Substitute fulfilling the role of another (9)
7 Imaginary paradise on earth (7-2)
11 Feudal superior (5,4)
12 Gobsmacked (9)
13 Fabric (5)
14 Produced from milk (5)
18 Language saying one thing but implying the opposite (6)
19 Offshoot (6)
22 Style of jazz (4)
23 Taverns (4)

Solution see page 269

146

ACROSS

1 Angst-ridden (9)
8 Raise up (5)
9 Disinters (7)
10 Room equipped with sunbeds (8)
11 Lean (4)
13 Charm (6)
14 Soak (6)
16 Pastry in very thin sheets (4)
17 Facial hair (8)
19 Large structure (7)
20 Short melody (5)
21 Indigestion (9)

DOWN

1 Seminar (8)
2 Penitent (6)
3 Resound (4)
4 Long established (4-8)
5 Let down (12)
6 Heretics fled (anag) — Derbyshire town with a crooked church spire (12)
7 Wastes time by being indecisive (5-7)
12 Hot drink — teenager (anag) (5,3)
15 Arm muscle (6)
18 Wind instrument (4)

Solution see page 269

147

ACROSS

1 Cut in two (6)

4 Aspect (5)

7 Partially fermented fodder (6)

8 Recline in a very relaxed manner (6)

9 Gamble (4)

10 4 of 64 or 5 of 125, for example (4,4)

12 Amusement — trouble (3,3,5)

17 Gorbachev's 'openness' (8)

19 Praise (4)

20 Charge with a crime (6)

21 Supporting beam over a door (6)

22 From this time (5)

23 Strike out (6)

DOWN

1 Landlord's agent (7)

2 Loosen — become less busy (7)

3 Increase in loudness (9)

4 Suddenly stood motionless (5)

5 Comfort (7)

6 Short internet messages (6)

11 Unimportant thing (9)

13 From an East African country? (7)

14 Assortment (7)

15 Extract juice from an orange, say (7)

16 Cruel and terrifying (6)

18 Recess — suitable position (5)

Solution see page 269

148

ACROSS

1 Where a compass needle points (8,5)
8 Hard-shelled seed (3)
9 Elephantine nose (9)
10 Strong and sporty (8)
11 Therefore (4)
13 Resist (6)
14 Effervescent (6)
16 Disgusting! (4)
17 Bend forward in pain or laughter (6,2)
20 Unhealthy interest in sexual matters (9)
21 Equipment (3)
22 In impressive style (13)

DOWN

1 Passion — mood disorder (5)
2 Understand a situation (3,3,7)
3 Coffee type (8)
4 Mockingly humorous (6)
5 Sheltered and secluded place (4)
6 Best-ever performance achiever (6–7)
7 Time passed (7)
12 Exercising weight (4-4)
13 Home of the Greek gods (7)
15 Brandy (6)
18 Infant's loo (5)
19 Winnow out (4)

Solution see page 269

149

ACROSS

1 Add on at the end (6)
4 Go faster, horsey! (3,2)
7 Give birth to piglets (6)
8 Stylish (6)
9 Disgusting waste matter (4)
10 Firmly tethered (8)
12 What holds the main microchips in a computer (11)
17 Superior skill (8)
19 Heavy dull sound (4)
20 Petrol jelly used in flame-throwers (6)
21 Supernatural (6)
22 Sexually attractive? (5)
23 Vanquish (6)

DOWN

1 A ragman (anag) (7)
2 Gemstone — pre-do it (anag) (7)
3 Guardian seller? (9)
4 Diagram showing the relationship between variable quantities (5)
5 Sovereign (7)
6 Ceremonial procession (6)
11 Place for keeping bits and bobs (9)
13 Sea creature's tentacles served as food (7)
14 'The', definitely (7)
15 Pair of similar things (7)
16 Hard dark-brown wood used for furniture (6)
18 With a smooth, gleaming surface (5)

Solution see page 270

150

ACROSS

1 Radiant — clever (6)
4 Vinegary (6)
8 Thin biscuit (5)
9 Make stronger (7)
10 In a moderately slow tempo (7)
11 Say baa! (5)
12 One who talks in an offensive way (9)
17 Muse of love poetry (5)
19 Edible root, eaten cooked — fils, say (anag) (7)
21 Hard-wearing twilled cloth — it's faun (anag) (7)
22 Glasses (abbr) (5)
23 Coming from Aden? (6)
24 Small animal with a pouch (6)

DOWN

1 Archer (6)
2 Unbeliever (7)
3 Wading bird (5)
5 North American reindeer (7)
6 Very short time (5)
7 North American wild dog (6)
9 Forenames (anag) (9))
13 Perfect (7)
14 Woman likely to succeed? (7)
15 Launch an attack on someone, verbally (3,3)
16 Mineral used to make plaster of Paris (6)
18 Tea-growing state in north-east India (5)
20 Cattle-catching rope (5)

Solution see page 270

151

ACROSS

1 Not on your nelly! (2,4)
4 Hindu retreat (6)
9 Flat surface forming the back of a boat (7)
10 Self-contained and specialised part of an animal (5)
11 Basis of a screwdriver (5)
12 Italian rice dish (7)
13 In a tent (5,6)
18 Small axe (7)
20 Area of swampy ground (5)
22 Juicy edible gourd (5)
23 Anthology of articles on a related subject (7)
24 Oliver Twist's friend, the Artful ___ (6)
25 Made warm (6)

DOWN

1 Indigenous (6)
2 Criminal deception (5)
3 Mitigate — allay (7)
5 Retail outlets (5)
6 Races for boats (7)
7 Very small fish (6)
8 Liquid rubbed into the skin (11)
14 Irritated (7)
15 Chosen candidate (7)
16 Dishonoured (6)
17 Pursued (6)
19 For this reason (5)
21 Someone who appears to have no emotions (5)

Solution see page 270

152

ACROSS

1 Parched (2,3,2,4)
9 Agitated (2,7)
10 Spoil (3)
11 Led an (anag) — antelope (5)
13 Long-lasting — sea legs (anag) (7)
14 Trouble constantly (6)
15 Bring to an end (6)
18 Sirius (3,4)
20 Lobster or crab roe (5)
21 Descendant (3)
22 Absolve (9)
24 Formally submitted (4,3,4)

DOWN

2 Pose for an artist (3)
3 Ornamental screen behind a church altar (7)
4 Hooded waterproof jacket (6)
5 Musical instruction to play gently and sweetly (5)
6 Wine steward (9)
7 Perish (4,3,4)
8 Skid lid (5,6)
12 Overbearing pride (9)
16 Under control (2,5)
17 Ornamental clasp (6)
19 Pay for — minister to — deal with (5)
23 Reverential fear (3)

Solution see page 270

153

ACROSS

1 Perimeter (13)

8 Oarsmen (anag) — Italian Riviera resort (7)

9 Fragment (5)

10 Audibly (or visually) obtrusive (4)

11 Over (8)

13 Writer (6)

14 Inborn (6)

17 Misadventure (8)

19 Storage space under a roof (4)

21 Cause annoyance (5)

22 Rectangles (7)

24 In a safe location (3,2,5,3)

DOWN

1 Type of lettuce (3)

2 French car manufacturer (7)

3 Functions (4)

4 Gambol (6)

5 Muscovites etc — as in USSR (anag) (8)

6 Compass bearing (5)

7 Means to an end (9)

10 Tibetan breed of dog (5,4)

12 Thin sheet of precious metal (4,4)

15 At present — from this moment onwards (2,2,3)

16 Breed of goat or rabbit (6)

18 Top of a wave (5)

20 Morose (4)

23 Sneaky (3)

Solution see page 271

154

ACROSS

5 In a difficult situation — under siege (11)

7 Long hard journey on foot (4)

8 Brief and precise (8)

9 Whim (7)

11 Passenger vessel operating on a regular schedule (5)

13 City in Somerset (5)

14 Produce a regular throbbing sensation (7)

16 Roman silver coin — is unread (anag) (8)

17 Pointed front part of a ship (4)

18 It let losers (anag) — spread rumours (4,7)

DOWN

1 Anti-aircraft fire (4)

2 Ankle-length garment worn by priests and choristers (7)

3 Inkling (5)

4 Ruffians (8)

5 Mourning (11)

6 Commemorative awards (11)

10 Trusty (8)

12 US detective (informal) (7)

15 Booth (5)

17 Straight-laced (4)

Solution see page 271

155

ACROSS

1 Flowering (2,5)

8 Arabian Nights hero (3,4)

9 Out of control (7)

10 Announce vehemently (7)

11 Wild dog (5)

13 Custody (9)

15 Place used secretly as a refuge (4,5)

18 Correct (5)

21 Married (anag) — lover (7)

22 Gourmet (7)

23 Large and brightly coloured handkerchief (7)

24 One failing to keep up (7)

DOWN

1 Secure firmly (5)

2 Chemical element, B (5)

3 A drink before departure (3,3,3,4)

4 Get there (4,2)

5 Causing one to feel unsettled (13)

6 Trip to see wild animals (6)

7 Smoked pig meat (6)

12 Notion (4)

14 Solemn promise (4)

15 Run down (6)

16 Livid (6)

17 Illusory (6)

19 Dutch cheese (5)

20 Scottish and English river (5)

Solution see page 271

156

ACROSS

1 California desert resort (4,7)

9 Tentative suggestions (9)

10 Precursor of the euro (3)

11 South American dance (5)

13 Delicate handling of a situation (7)

14 Street performer (6)

15 Band of warriors (6)

18 Pain — a bum log (anag) (7)

20 Canadian territory, famed for the 1897 gold rush (5)

21 Heath or Hughes? (3)

22 Charlie Parker's 'horn'? (9)

24 Rich sponge (7,4)

DOWN

2 Get rid of (3)

3 Greenhouse gas produced by cows (7)

4 Rid of intrusive substances (6)

5 Author of Peer Gynt (5)

6 Supposition (9)

7 Likelihood (11)

8 Nature's perk (anag) — vessel (11)

12 TV, papers etc (4,5)

16 Of Summer or Winter games (7)

17 Trick player (6)

19 Side passage (5)

23 Hard durable wood of a deciduous tree (3)

Solution see page 271

157

ACROSS

1 Largest Caribbean island (4)

3 Sparkling wine (slang) (8)

9 Crossbred hunting dog (7)

10 Moderate glow (5)

11 Comply with (3,2)

12 Sway, as if about to fall (6)

14 Very close by (2,3,8)

17 Medium of divine revelation (6)

19 Slow speech with prolonged vowels (5)

22 Obliterate (5)

23 Meeting of a court (7)

24 Sauce for salad (8)

25 Outdoor festivity (4)

DOWN

1 Vocal ads (anag) — apple brandy (8)

2 Soft cap (5)

4 British admiral d. 21 October 1805 (7,6)

5 Strength (5)

6 Constituent — habitat (7)

7 Japanese wrestling (4)

8 As a consequence (6)

13 Conspicuous wealth (8)

15 Mayonnaise-based sauce with capers, eaten with fish (7)

16 Red cold salad ingredient (6)

18 Green cold salad ingredient (5)

20 Spry (5)

21 Be in want of (4)

Solution see page 272

158

ACROSS

1 Spiritedness (8)

5 50% (4)

9 Melodic (5)

10 Packed crowd of people (7)

11 Sea south of Texas (4,2,6)

13 Sharp vibrating sounds (6)

14 Butt of jokes (6)

17 No! — get out with you! (1,4,5,2)

20 Seafarer (7)

21 Sieved food reduced to pulp (5)

22 Support for putting things on (4)

23 In perfect health (4,4)

DOWN

1 Long depression containing a river (4)

2 Wart on the foot (7)

3 Illicit blood sport involving birds (12)

4 Inside information (3-3)

6 Old calculators (5)

7 Small dugouts for protection from hostile fire (8)

8 Get a move on! (4,2,6)

12 Hand-held grass cutter (8)

15 See (7)

16 Price for a service (6)

18 Monsters (5)

19 Lock-up room (4)

Solution see page 272

159

ACROSS

1 Six-sided dehydrated block used in cooking (5,4)

8 Intangible quality surrounding a person or thing (4)

9 Time immemorial (9)

10 Evidence of an old injury (4)

13 Check the growth of (something) (5)

15 Deep-fried potato outlet (6)

16 Royal guard (6)

17 Important person (6)

19 Fatigue after a long-haul flight (3,3)

20 Tile fixer (5)

21 Note (4)

24 Ecstatic (4-1-4)

25 Mild yellow Dutch cheese (4)

26 Spirit of a generation (9)

DOWN

2 Water reservoir (4)

3 Penny, say? (4)

4 Shire (6)

5 Plant study (6)

6 Avocado dip (9)

7 Condescension (9)

11 Holder of frozen water (3,6)

12 Imaginary stringed instrument (3,6)

13 Twig (5)

14 Key principle (5)

18 Long narrow furrow (6)

19 Official trip at public expense? (6)

22 I'm going downhill, fast! (4)

23 Small green flowerless plant (4)

Solution see page 272

160

ACROSS

1 Skill with a blade (13)
8 Choose not to vote (7)
9 Social customs (5)
10 Title given in parts of Asia to important people (4)
11 Second-largest Mediterranean island, after Sicily (8)
13 Descendant of French settlers in Louisiana (6)
14 Back scrubber (6)
17 Rep (8)
19 Norwegian city, formerly Kristiania (4)
21 Irk (5)
22 Set on fire (7)
24 Severe reprimand (6-7)

DOWN

1 Salt water (3)
2 Visible to the theatre audience (7)
3 Having two distinct functions (4)
4 Handbook (6)
5 Casually mention famous people you know (4-4)
6 Great Lake (5)
7 Green nut (9)
10 Stimulate (4-5)
12 Gesundheit! (5,3)
15 Spiral pasta (7)
16 Wild dog-like animal (6)
18 Cloth made from flax (5)
20 Social insects (4)
23 Turn up earth (3)

Solution see page 272

161

ACROSS

1 Ridiculous combination of two figures of speech (5,8)
8 Gob (4)
9 Scornfully mocking (8)
10 Unquenchable (10)
12 Yes-man (6)
14 Champagne (informal) (6)
15 Financial security — teeters, say (anag) (4,6)
19 Large church building (8)
20 Early stringed instrument (4)
21 Clean-and-jerk sport (13)

DOWN

2 Exemption from punishment (8)
3 Additional (5)
4 Projectile (sometimes guided) (7)
5 Palpitate (5)
6 Adage (7)
7 Roman poet, d. about AD17 (4)
11 Lunar occurrence (which almost never happens) (4,4)
13 First — beginning (7)
14 Kind of long-grained rice (7)
16 Canonised person (5)
17 Fasten — engross (5)
18 Open jar for holding flowers (4)

Solution see page 273

162

ACROSS

1 Knock off (6)
4 Detestable (6)
9 Small cube of fried bread (7)
10 Ate (5)
11 Make painstaking enquiries (into something) (5)
12 Kill (7)
13 By its very nature (11)
18 Pig hurt (anag) — noble (7)
20 Lacerate (5)
22 Alec's (anag) — graduation (5)
23 Malicious hostility (7)
24 Mankind (6)
25 Scurry — small car (6)

DOWN

1 Reach a conclusion (6)
2 Whimsically comical (5)
3 Road safety device (7)
5 Needless (5)
6 Voluptuous (7)
7 Progress unsteadily (due to age?) (6)
8 Ceremony of conferring honours of rank on a person (11)
14 Bitter derision (7)
15 Failure to be there (7)
16 Sudden illegal acquisition of power (6)
17 Accumulation of electricity (6)
19 Envious — environmentalist (5)
21 Take as one's own (5)

Solution see page 273

163

ACROSS

1 Dreadful (4)
3 Overshadowed (8)
9 Unfavourable (7)
10 Talk show group (5)
11 Abatement (3-2)
12 Allotted amount (6)
14 Hong Kong airline (6,7)
17 Medical facility (6)
19 Achieve great things (2,3)
22 Spare tyre location? (5)
23 Peeved (2,1,4)
24 Spanish cheese — come hang (anag) (8)
25 Boxing match signal (4)

DOWN

1 Stalemate (8)
2 Metal fastener (5)
4 Selecting only the best (6-7)
5 Provision of data (5)
6 Farewell celebration (4-3)
7 Unemployment benefit (4)
8 Italian brandy (6)
13 Contemptuous (8)
15 Capital on the Gulf of Finland (7)
16 French brandy (6)
18 Nick (5)
20 Accidental success (5)
21 Bathe (4)

Solution see page 273

164

ACROSS

1 Charades, for example (7,4)
9 Embedded (9)
10 Junk (3)
11 Soil's organic component (5)
13 Ledger for recording transactions as they occur (7)
14 Sudden arrival (of people or water?) (6)
15 Kiss and cuddle (6)
18 US state — Black Sea state (7)
20 Regal (5)
21 Sign of the zodiac (3)
22 Large broad-bladed weapon (9)
24 Men's underwear (5,6)

DOWN

2 Snake (3)
3 Negotiates between parties (7)
4 Disordered (6)
5 Devout (5)
6 Legends and sagas, in general (9)
7 The Lady with the Lamp, d. 1910 (11)
8 Person or organisation with an interest in something (11)
12 Venetian travel writer, who may (or may not) have served Kublai Khan, d. 1324 (5,4)
16 Dark cherry (7)
17 Carnivorous insect, which rests as if in prayer (6)
19 Part between sloping sides of a roof (5)
23 Relevant (3)

Solution see page 273

165

ACROSS

1 Anything could now happen! (3,4,3,3)

8 The Thames at Oxford (4)

9 If absolutely necessary (2,1,5)

10 ESP (5,5)

12 (Self-appointed) expert (6)

14 Ancillaries (6)

15 Early instrument like a piano — rich oval CD (anag) (10)

19 Possess some similarity to (8)

20 Right-hand man/woman (4)

21 Lake in Hyde Park (3,10)

DOWN

2 Juicy (8)

3 Surround and harass (5)

4 Passage (7)

5 Once more (5)

6 Illustrious (7)

7 Countenance (4)

11 Virago — rain hard (anag) (8)

13 Author of Our Mutual Friend, d. 1870 (7)

14 Stare with the power to harm? (4,3)

16 Light colour between red and green (5)

17 Earth (anag) — compassion (5)

18 Amphetamine taken as a stimulant (4)

Solution see page 274

166

ACROSS

1 Turning point on which important developments depend (4)

3 Of the chest (8)

9 One who gives up too easily (7)

10 Briefs of two small panels connected by strings (5)

11 Complete (5)

12 In truth (6)

14 Lying between huge collections of stars — a critical gent (anag) (13)

17 Speak indistinctly (6)

19 Revise (3,2)

22 Little, charming and naughty (5)

23 Parthenogenetic (7)

24 Express grumpy opposition (8)

25 Small keyboarding error (4)

DOWN

1 Casserole of chicken pieces and onions in red wine (3,2,3)

2 Try to avoid (a problem) (5)

4 Oil-fuelled light with a glass chimney for outdoor use (9,4)

5 Highly valued (5)

6 Agreement (7)

7 Scuttler (4)

8 One gazing intently (6)

13 Mexican Pacific resort (8)

15 Until now (4,3)

16 Band worn for decoration (6)

18 Language group of southern Africa (5)

20 Flashy (5)

21 Netting (4)

Solution see page 274

167

ACROSS

5 Things are just as bad for me! (4,3,4)

7 Complacent (4)

8 Patty of shredded seafood and mashed potato (8)

9 Cool dude (7)

11 I beg your pardon (5)

13 Softly radiant (5)

14 State of being under arrest (7)

16 Salmon-like fish that also migrates from salt to fresh water (3,5)

17 Champagne, say? (4)

18 Shoving it in (anag) — cat-like ability? (5,6)

DOWN

1 Vitality (4)

2 Full of food (7)

3 From Swansea, say? (5)

4 Momentary loss of consciousness (8)

5 Moving seed of a Mexican shrub containing larva of a moth (7,4)

6 13 (6,5)

10 Lack (8)

12 Refuse container (7)

15 Cubicle (5)

17 Secret departure (by moonlight?) (4)

Solution see page 274

168

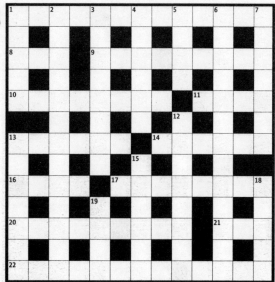

ACROSS

1 Japanese professional sport — mustering owls (anag) (4,9)
8 Pro (3)
9 Before league games begin (9)
10 Norwegian polar explorer, d. 1928 (8)
11 Hurt (4)
13 Keep silent (4,2)
14 Walkout (6)
16 Appearance (4)
17 Gob (informal) (8)
20 Logic (9)
21 Eccentric (3)
22 Horse that jumps (13)

DOWN

1 Bulgarian capital (5)
2 French libertine, d. 1814 (7,2,4)
3 Obliterated (5,3)
4 1 and 1? (6)
5 Youth (4)
6 Having a diet of ants etc (13)
7 From the capital of the Liguria region of Italy (7)
12 Potency (8)
13 Arm bone (7)
15 Dog — tooth (6)
18 Type of duck (5)
19 Liquid food (4)

Solution see page 274

169

ACROSS

1 Patellae (8)
5 Snoopy's imprecation (4)
9 Glandular organ in the abdomen (5)
10 Prove superior (7)
11 Without warning (3,2,1,6)
13 Attribute (6)
14 Save from peril (6)
17 Called to remembrance (12)
20 Fashionable — served with ice cream (1,2,4)
21 Lay to rest (5)
22 Long protruding tooth (4)
23 Soaked by rain (8)

DOWN

1 Hardy cabbage (4)
2 Surround completely (7)
3 Maize eaten as a vegetable (4,2,3,3)
4 Tree — London district (6)
6 Prize (5)
7 Small, sharp sliver (8)
8 Money paid for work or a service (12)
12 Flying machine (8)
15 Fastest land animal (7)
16 Peeping Tom (6)
18 Resources (5)
19 Poke (4)

Solution see page 275

170

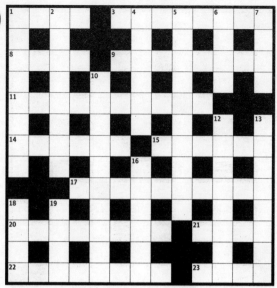

ACROSS

1 Short, light breath of wind (4)

3 Nous (8)

8 Marching orders? (4)

9 Gritty (like some sugar?) (8)

11 Involving very poor social conditions — case in kind (anag) (10)

14 Mechanical force causing rotation (6)

15 Mexican cocktail made with white rum and lime juice (6)

17 Regardless (5–5)

20 Morning call (8)

21 Cain's younger brother (4)

22 The 'John' of 'John Smith' (8)

23 Summons (4)

DOWN

1 Assign to a later time (8)

2 Queen or Jack, say? (4,4)

4 Agitation (6)

5 Baggy trousers gathered at the ankles (10)

6 Ailments — misfortunes (4)

7 Informer (4)

10 Person giving hair and skin treatments etc (10)

12 Atmospheric pressure unit (8)

13 Speaker of many languages (8)

16 Downhill ski event (6)

18 High-ranking university academic (abbr) (4)

19 Six balls, as a unit (4)

Solution see page 275

171

ACROSS

1 Bavarian shorts with braces (10)

7 Candid (7)

8 North American plant with swordshaped leaves (5)

10 Coughs up (4)

11 Not in keeping with accepted standards (8)

13 Hurry (6)

15 Suddenly go berserk (4,2)

17 Lovely (8)

18 Imitate — a nymph (4)

21 Well known (5)

22 Put at risk (7)

23 Selfishly, just take the best bits (6-4)

DOWN

1 Tall (5)

2 Arab lateen-rigged sailing ship (4)

3 Score (6)

4 Contradictory figure of speech (8)

5 Small territory completely surrounded by another one (7)

6 Start too quickly (4,3,3)

9 Tried out for a part (10)

12 Back (8)

14 Time period (7)

16 Provide with goods (6)

19 Make a sound like a hen (5)

20 (Person who is) not in favour (4)

Solution see page 275

172

ACROSS

1 Shortcoming (10)
7 The First State (to ratify the US constitution) (8)
8 Sly look (4)
9 Unpleasantly moist (4)
10 Losing one's hair (7)
12 In unison (3,8)
14 Curtains (7)
16 Stretch over (4)
19 Clubs (4)
20 Disease — a side bet (anag) (8)
21 With great courage (10)

DOWN

1 Great fear (5)
2 Facecloth (7)
3 Applaud (4)
4 Lofty (8)
5 Managed well enough (5)
6 More eager (6)
11 Passage (8)
12 Out of the country (6)
13 Unlucky — he slaps (anag) (7)
15 Outdated (5)
17 Poor (5)
18 Plinth (4)

Solution see page 275

173

ACROSS

5 Prize for last place (6,5)
7 Rum and water (4)
8 Private (8)
9 Pickled cucumber (7)
11 Buxom (5)
13 Emblem (5)
14 Rubbers (7)
16 Of the highest qualiy (8)
17 Snob (4)
18 Nonsense (6,5)

DOWN

1 Medal (4)
2 Swimming costume (3,4)
3 Fraud — dupes (anag) (5)
4 State of stagnation (8)
5 Kindly (4-7)
6 Manicurist's cosmetic (4,7)
10 Leaving no stone unturned (8)
12 Army grouping (7)
15 Female horse under four years old (5)
17 Sympathy and sorrow (4))

Solution see page 276

174

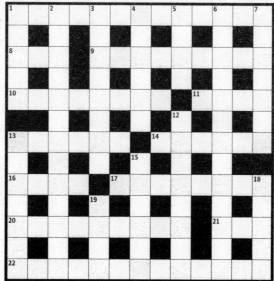

ACROSS

1 A who's-the-daddy action (9,4)
8 Shoulder-to-wrist member (3)
9 Stewed meat in a thick white sauce (9)
10 Obsessed with a single subject (3-5)
11 Not a sausage (4)
13 Postpone (3,3)
14 Human (6)
16 Salmon-coloured (4)
17 Flat-sided fuel carrier (5,3)
20 Cantankerous (9)
21 Romanian money (3)
22 Building between The Mall and Trafalgar Square (9,4)

DOWN

1 Instrument with ivories (5)
2 Hissy fit (6,7)
3 Undesirable people (4-4)
4 Folly (6)
5 Chinese money (4)
6 Ordinary (13)
7 Loftier (anag) — clover-like plant (7)
12 Good manners (8)
13 Powdered hot spice (7)
15 Communicated in words (6)
18 Horse sound (5)
19 Actor in a principal role (4)

Solution see page 276

175

ACROSS

1 Mucky (6)
4 Circulate (6)
9 Branch off (7)
10 Promotional guff (5)
11 Communications medium (5)
12 Because of that (7)
13 Loo (5,6)
18 Expressing deep emotion (7)
20 What proverbially follows day (5)
22 Light semi-transparent fabric (5)
23 Supermarket vehicle (7)
24 Spin (6)
25 Comparatively near (6)

DOWN

1 Felt hat with a creased crown (6)
2 Furious (5)
3 Secretion from an endocrine gland (7)
5 Permeate (5)
6 Whole-milk holey cheese (7)
7 Fertilised human egg (6)
8 Sign (11)
14 Fly people and goods to places not otherwise accessible (7)
15 Score at the wrong end (3,4)
16 Dribble (6)
17 Horse (or person) that can go the distance (6)
19 Chin split (5)
21 Government fixed-interest securities — young sows (5)

Solution see page 276

176

ACROSS

1 Pool for performing marine mammals (12)

9 Paved area outside a house (5)

10 Sharp — indicated (7)

11 Teaching both girls and boys (2-2)

12 One way of scoring at rugby (4,4)

14 Unhealthy looking (6)

15 C–F musical interval — Prince Regent George's eventual regnal number (6)

18 Lacking written authentication? (8)

20 All Blacks' war dance (4)

22 Clump of grass (7)

23 Pale brownish-yellow colour (5)

24 Plan to get out! (4,8)

DOWN

2 Ground grain used to make porridge (7)

3 Classical music concert for which part of the audience stands (4)

4 Communicate (6)

5 Political propaganda in art or literature (8)

6 First part of a news story (abbr) (5)

7 Confused (6-6)

8 Reusable rocket-launched craft flown by astronauts (5,7)

13 Powerful infantry weapons used against the French at Agincourt, 1415 (8)

16 Selfish and dangerous driver (4,3)

17 Plastic cup without a handle (6)

19 Cold rice balls with raw fish (5)

21 Handgun — young horse (4)

Solution see page 276

177

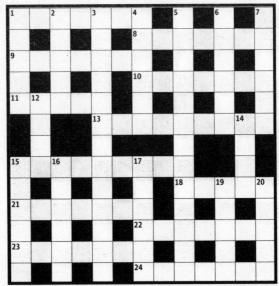

ACROSS

1 Circular (7)

8 Inspiring fear (7)

9 Kite ban (anag) — bohemian (7)

10 Apostolic letter (7)

11 Long-handled spoon for serving soup (5)

13 No longer scheduled (9)

15 Revive (something) (9)

18 Turn aside (5)

21 Person keeping watch (7)

22 Sent out (7)

23 Waterfall (7)

24 Dog of mixed breed (7)

DOWN

1 Defamation (5)

2 Give, as an honour (5)

3 Junior NCO in the British Army (5,8)

4 Hire (4,2)

5 Strict organisation and control (13)

6 Building providing cheap overnight accommodation (6)

7 Stand up for (6)

12 Tool for shaping large pieces of wood (4)

14 Always (4)

15 Objects of historical interest (6)

16 Partner in marriage (6)

17 High regard (6)

19 Penetrate (5)

20 Ebbing and flowing (5)

Solution see page 277

178

ACROSS

1 Make someone feel let down (10)
7 Sumptuous and spacious (8)
8 Undressed (4)
9 In apple-pie order (4)
10 Censure severely (7)
12 Sordid gain (6,5)
14 Notice carried for public display (7)
16 Little lies (4)
19 Mane (4)
20 Hostile (8)
21 Tie the knot (3,7)

DOWN

1 Preliminary sketch (5)
2 Disgraceful event (7)
3 Claw (4)
4 Very unpleasant place (8)
5 Roman Catholic service read about 3pm (5)
6 Stick (6)
11 Surly (8)
12 As befitting one's daughter or son (6)
13 Gathering with Celtic folk music, singing and dancing (7)
15 Nobel Prize winner for physics (1903) and chemistry (1911), d. 1934 (5)
17 Piece of broken ceramic — London skyscraper (5)
18 Reject a lover without warning (4)

Solution see page 277

179

ACROSS

1 Trawler's catch (4)
3 Thick white sauce (8)
9 Daft (7)
10 Originally Russian spirit (5)
11 Run along now! (3,2)
12 Feeling of excitement (6)
14 Hard-headed (13)
17 Small group of like-minded politicians (6)
19 Civilian clothes worn by service personnel (5)
22 Arctic dwelling (5)
23 Someone unprepared to face the facts (7)
24 Independence (8)
25 Founder of Christian Science, d. 1910 (4)

DOWN

1 Item producing momentary light for taking a photograph (8)
2 Subsist on very little (5)
4 A highly charged disturbance? (8,5)
5 Hang in the air (5)
6 Estuary area flooded at high tide, uncovered at low (3,4)
7 Bound (4)
8 Fluffy little animal (6)
13 Huge (8)
15 Bright red (7)
16 Hostility (6)
18 Sing softly (5)
20 Cooked in oil (5)
21 Travel pass (4)

Solution see page 277

180

ACROSS

5 Clothes for casual activities (11)

7 Outlay (4)

8 Artificially high singing voice (8)

9 Judge to be probable (5,2)

11 Ruffle (5)

13 Fawn (5)

14 Thief (slang) (3,4)

16 Abuse (8)

17 Game counter representing money (4)

18 Believing in equal opportunities (11)

DOWN

1 Highland dress (4)

2 Clown (7)

3 Answer (5)

4 Intellectual (8)

5 Appear as old as one is (4,4,3)

6 Vengeance (11)

10 Drink before bedtime (8)

12 Supporting male actor at a wedding (4,3)

15 Moderately warm (5)

17 Metal currency (4)

Solution see page 277

181

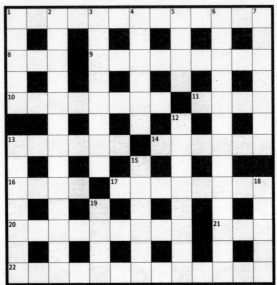

ACROSS

1 Ability in the management of national affairs (13)

8 Select as an alternative (3)

9 Reach adult status (4,2,3)

10 Read through briefly (4,4)

11 Item of footwear (4)

13 Amorous embrace? (6)

14 Dance around excitedly (6)

16 Patriarch who saved his family and all the animals from drowning (4)

17 Death (slang) (8)

20 Stirring — anxiety (9)

21 Star that provides light and heat for a solar system (3)

22 Absence (3-10)

DOWN

1 Seat without a back (5)

2 Oppressively strict (13)

3 Intrude gradually (8)

4 Person belonging to a particular group (6)

5 Midday (4)

6 Ridiculously over-complicated in design and/or construction (5,8)

7 Rule of conduct (7)

12 Secured (8)

13 Hold within (7)

15 Pointless (6)

18 From that time (5)

19 Handle of an axe (4)

Solution see page 278

182

ACROSS

1 Steak cut from between the ribs (9)

8 Therefore (4)

9 Reggae singer, guitarist and songwriter, d. 1981 (3,6)

10 Retained (4)

13 Beginning (5)

15 About 3,500,000 square miles of Africa (6)

16 Team sport, informally (6)

17 Sir Frederick __ , choreographer, d. 1988 (6)

19 Predicament (6)

20 Blue-blooded (5)

21 Head (slang) — be a slacker (4)

24 Finished (9)

25 Native wit (4)

26 Toiletry product (9)

DOWN

2 Gas — light (4)

3 City not built in a day (4)

4 Ring round the sun or moon (6)

5 Sway, as if about to fall (6)

6 Variety of plum (9)

7 Postgraduate degree (9)

11 Attacker (9)

12 Mexican state — breed of dog (9)

13 Synthetic acrylic fibre (5)

14 Fine net fabric (5)

18 Like a dead parrot? (2,4)

19 Situated (6)

22 Soft regional accent (4)

23 Spiteful — excellent (slang) (4)

Solution see page 278

183

ACROSS

5 Three-stringed instrument used to play Russian folk music (9)
8 Forearm bone (4)
9 Federal prison in California, 1934–63 (8)
10 Prone to chuckling (6)
11 One or the other (6)
13 Not a good person! (3,3)
15 Glitch (6)
16 Night light? (8)
18 Master (4)
19 Seemingly without limit (9)

DOWN

1 Tirade (8)
2 Bright yellow shade (6)
3 Lacking social polish (6)
4 Parody (4)
6 Croc's close relative (9)
7 Preserve (9)
12 (Of a problem) difficult to handle and requiring great tact (8)
14 The Quiet American author (6)
15 Lecture on a moral topic (6)
17 Gas used in fluorescent lighting (4)

Solution see page 278

184

ACROSS

1 Small auk (9)

8 Propelled like a Mediterranean war galley (5)

9 Somewhat less dirty (7)

10 Superficially appealing actions that make no sense (8)

11 Make a noise like a cat (4)

13 Fish hawk (6)

14 Make a noise like a dog (3-3)

16 Macbeth or The Caretaker, say? (4)

17 Large (royal?) crustacean (4,4)

19 With too much sound (7)

20 Notion of perfection (5)

21 Ridiculed satirically (9)

DOWN

1 Bon voyage! (8)

2 Experiences (6)

3 Onion-like vegetable (from Wales?) (4)

4 Kind of beet grown as cattle food — glum re Zen law (anag) (6-6)

5 Become irrationally angry or upset (informal) (5,1,6)

6 Flat surface having switches, dials and meters (7,5)

7 OTT celebration in victory (12)

12 Tuneful flyer (8)

15 From Benghazi? (6)

18 Main barrier island in the Venice Lagoon (4)

Solution see page 278

185

ACROSS

5 Statements about the future (11)

7 Wee drop of whisky? (4)

8 Thin slice of boneless meat (8)

9 Bound by oath (7)

11 Striped quadruped (5)

13 Fishing vessel (5)

14 Dull — commonplace (7)

16 Sick headache (8)

17 Elegantly stylish (4)

18 Minced meat in pastry snack (7,4)

DOWN

1 Smile radiantly (4)

2 Magi (4,3)

3 Lodged (5)

4 Coal miners (8)

5 International competition for disabled athletes (11)

6 Far from thorough (11)

10 Seemly (8)

12 Felt great sorrow (7)

15 King with the golden touch (5)

17 Dog — food (4)

Solution see page 279

186

ACROSS

1 At least half the time (2,5,2,3)
9 Edible fish (5)
10 Criminal gang member (7)
11 Young lady (4)
12 Asian part of Turkey (8)
14 Bavarian capital (6)
15 Language (6)
18 Young art (anag) — worthless (8)
20 Yellowish brown (4)
22 Popular 18th-century dance — vet goat (anag) (7)
23 Sports clothing material (5)
24 Specialised food shop (12)

DOWN

2 Pouch worn with a kilt (7)
3 Kismet (4)
4 Expensive white fur (6)
5 Cherished aspiration (8)
6 Relating to birth (5)
7 Refuse to listen (4,1,4,3)
8 Carefully arranged for a desired effect (5–7)
13 Deliriously happy (8)
16 Watercolour painting with opaque colours (7)
17 (In heraldry) silver (6)
19 Auctioneer's hammer (5)
21 Cry of woe (4)

Solution see page 279

187

ACROSS

1 Aromatic herb used as seasoning (4)

3 Sloppy (8)

9 Ice cream flavour (7)

10 Secure room — spring over (5)

11 Test(ing) of a substance, such as precious metal (5)

12 Fool (6)

14 Understanding (13)

17 Fasten securely (6)

19 Kind of crossing? (5)

22 Truth assumed to be self-evident (5)

23 Involving controversy — compile (anag) (7)

24 Woman on the prowl, like the goddess Diana? (8)

25 Open grassland of southern Africa (4)

DOWN

1 Aberration (8)

2 Connections (5)

4 Study how to do a job (5,3,5)

5 Swivel (5)

6 Escape artist, d. 1926 (7)

7 Sweet fruit with a long woody seed (4)

8 Actor — musician (6)

13 Improved (8)

15 Make reference to (7)

16 Rub noses (6)

18 Old Greek epic poet (5)

20 Dome-shaped dessert (5)

21 Whip (4)

Solution see page 279

188

ACROSS

5 Excessively large amount (11)
7 One of the seven deadly sins (4)
8 In an off-hand manner (8)
9 Loose-fitting dress without a waist (7)
11 Ice cream portion (5)
13 Extra payment (5)
14 Minerva, for example (7)
16 Bat-and-ball game (8)
17 Make a reservation (4)
18 Unit of area (6,5)

DOWN

1 Remove the ovaries of a female animal (4)
2 Exact (7)
3 Partially melted snow (5)
4 Paid for (8)
5 Occurring at the same time (11)
6 First US national park, 1872 (11)
10 Lugubrious (8)
12 Disgusting — ie moons (anag) (7)
15 Acquire knowledge (5)
17 Wagers (4)

Solution see page 279

189

ACROSS

1 One who owes money (6)

4 Alcoholic pick-me-up (6)

9 One Ford (anag) — ruined (4,3)

10 Part of the cricket wicket (5)

11 Promiscuous (5)

12 Set going (7)

13 Ruse designed to disguise one's real intentions (11)

18 Inner distinctive nature of anything (7)

20 Step (5)

22 Person acting as a judge? (5)

23 Catastrophic (7)

24 Depict artistically (6)

25 Courteously (6)

DOWN

1 Deprive by deceit (6)

2 Stringed instrument (5)

3 At a time when demand is less (3-4)

5 Disprove (5)

6 Short section of sharp bends on a motor-racing track (7)

7 More impetuous — slice of meat (6)

8 Full-bodied sweet fortified wine (5,6)

14 Assignment — calling (7)

15 Italian operatic composer, d. 1868 (7)

16 Person who rouses game birds to be shot (6)

17 Liking to wear fancy or formal clothes (6)

19 Treat carefully (5)

21 Got up (5)

Solution see page 280

190

ACROSS

1 Hot breakfast food (8)
5 Smear (4)
9 Egyptian peninsula (5)
10 Rattle (7)
11 Daring and romantic adventurer (12)
13 Unspecified person (6)
14 Foot-operated boat (6)
17 Too informally clothed for the occasion (12)
20 Metal cutter (7)
21 Loud and rude (5)
22 Affectedly creative (4)
23 Stupid (8)

DOWN

1 Upper-class (4)
2 Absconder (7)
3 Foible (12)
4 Soiled (6)
6 Start of the financial year (5)
7 Purple vegetable (8)
8 Difficult to reach (12)
12 Elderly Russian woman (8)
15 Norm (7)
16 Gardener's tool (6)
18 Old gold coin (5)
19 Units of electrical resistance (4)

Solution see page 280

191

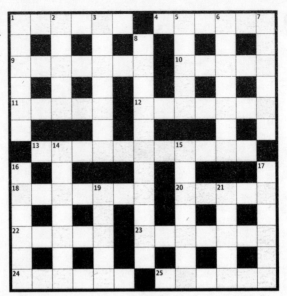

ACROSS

1 Please (anag) — pass away (6)
4 Prohibited (6)
9 Master of ceremonies (7)
10 Hulking (5)
11 French oil and gas company (5)
12 Time of full daylight (7)
13 Spell — delight (11)
18 Open-minded (7)
20 Plunge into water (5)
22 (Of writing paper) having printed lines (5)
23 Sleeveless pullover (4,3)
24 Result (anag) — gloss (6)
25 Unnatural lack of skin colour (6)

DOWN

1 Act as a stimulant (6)
2 Let in (5)
3 Furtiveness (7)
5 Drained of colour (5)
6 Hoodlum (7)
7 English poet, d. 1700 (6)
8 Charisma (11)
14 Small savoury snacks (7)
15 Representation of the Virgin Mary (7)
16 Composed of more than one (6)
17 Capsicum (6)
19 Person in the saddle (5)
21 Up to (5)

Solution see page 280

192

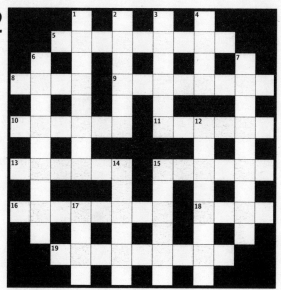

ACROSS

5 Emotionally upset — worried (9)
8 Quote (4)
9 Medieval musician (8)
10 Order to come (6)
11 Protect(ion) (6)
13 Without delay (2,4)
15 Contaminate (6)
16 Those on our side? (4,4)
18 Nautical pole (4)
19 Comically ugly (9)

DOWN

1 Churchwarden's assistant — semi-sand (anag) (8)
2 Pollen-producing part of a flower (6)
3 Tricks (6)
4 Deal with — encounter (4)
6 State of affairs — job (9)
7 Aggressive and ready to fight (9)
12 Notorious (8)
14 Even-handedness (6)
15 Demand firmly (6)
17 Sudden quick movement (4)

Solution see page 280

193

ACROSS

5 Unclear one way or the other (9)

8 Framework holding window panes (4)

9 Seducer (8)

10 Bootlick (6)

11 Brownish–red apple (6)

13 Summary (6)

15 The 'ly' of 'badly'? (6)

16 Moribund (8)

18 Be in a huff (4)

19 Lengthy procedure (9)

DOWN

1 Forceful (8)

2 Surge (6)

3 Talk under one's breath (6)

4 Brass instrument (4)

6 Preferred (9)

7 Danger zone (9)

12 Gently persuasive marketing (4,4)

14 Unpleasantly suave (6)

15 Planet with rings (6)

17 Guts and gumption (4)

Solution see page 281

194

ACROSS

1 Set of drawers for documents (6,7)

8 Toy percussion instrument — mid-turn (anag) (3,4)

9 Dwarfs or deadly sins? (5)

10 (Be in) a huff (4)

11 Scouts or Guides rally (8)

13 Payment for use — antler (anag) (6)

14 -ly word (6)

17 Sameness (8)

19 Trick (4)

21 Hawaiian hello (5)

22 Cutting wood (7)

24 Sudden intense excitement (7,6)

DOWN

1 Healthy (3)

2 Ointment containing wool fat (7)

3 Typical pattern (4)

4 Crashing instrument (6)

5 Meddler (8)

6 On no occasion (5)

7 Volatile situation (9)

10 Rugby player — March's flu (anag) (5,4)

12 Seasoned smoked beef, served in thin slices (8)

15 Gradual wearing away (7)

16 Disconnect (kettle or toaster?) (6)

18 Loop in a rope made with a slip knot (5)

20 Food thickening agent obtained from seaweed (4)

23 Man (3)

Solution see page 281

195

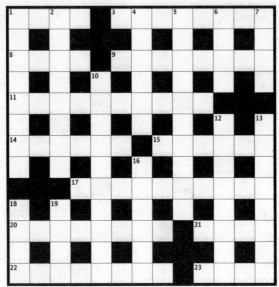

ACROSS

1 Sound made by a dog (4)
3 Dropping of flakes (8)
8 Bound (4)
9 Duke of Marlborough's seat at Woodstock (8)
11 Affectedly genteel (5-5)
14 Distinctive uniform (6)
15 Hidden marksman (6)
17 Burly chassis for Shirley Bassey, say? (10)
20 Flat Italian bread made with olive oil (8)
21 Yugoslav marshall, prime minister and president, d. 1980 (4)
22 Wrist ornament (8)
23 Cruel and wicked person (4)

DOWN

1 Refuge (8)
2 Stay of execution (8)
4 Emma Hamilton's lover, who died in battle on 21 October 1805 (6)
5 Structure for testing aircraft parts by blowing air over them (4,6)
6 Again but differently (4)
7 Compact mass (4)
10 Boat that lifts out of the water at high speeds (10)
12 Organised opposition to authority (8)
13 Woodland plant with yellow flowers in spring (8)
16 Baby's sock-like shoe (6)
18 Crust over a wound (4)
19 Long involved story (4)

Solution see page 281

196

ACROSS

1 Pasta dish (from an Italian city) (9)

8 A half-crown? (5)

9 Bar (7)

10 Rules of furniture arrangement — huge fins (anag) (4,4)

11 Seed carrying pod with hooks (4)

13 Long cream puff (6)

14 See you! (3–3)

16 Father (4)

17 Knickers (8)

19 Rock from which a metal can be extracted (4,3)

20 Throw (5)

21 Insipid (9)

DOWN

1 Busby (8)

2 Type of shoe (4-2)

3 Stick(er) (4)

4 Make a humiliating apology (3,6,3)

5 VDU information that something's wrong (5,7)

6 Pompous bore (7,5)

7 Self-important — savouring oil (anag) (12)

12 Précis (8)

15 Covering for an arm (6)

18 Set of rules (4)

Solution see page 281

197

ACROSS

1 Controversial issue attracting public attention (5,7)

9 Granny Smith, for one (5)

10 Type of lettuce (7)

11 Lie to get something (4)

12 Building divided into small let units (8)

14 Playing a part (6)

15 Sheep from Spain with a heavy quality fleece (6)

18 Latest time for completion (8)

20 Flower — girl (4)

22 Florida resort — Virginia Woolf novel (7)

23 Heavy iron-bound stick used for crowd control by police in India (5)

24 Canadian province (3,9)

DOWN

2 Road-surfacing material (7)

3 Outhouse — cast (4)

4 Bird with a long curved bill (6)

5 Palm tree (anag) — south Wales university town (8)

6 Groom's partner (5)

7 Method for removing unwanted hair (12)

8 Devoted old married couple (5,3,4)

13 Quick joke (3–5)

16 Crackbrained (7)

17 In utero (6)

19 Acknowledge — concede (5)

21 Defect (4)

Solution see page 282

198

ACROSS

1 Blameless — totally honest (5,8)
8 Mark left by a wound (4)
9 Like new (8)
10 Large fly — wild cornflower (10)
12 Maintain formally (6)
14 Alkali-metal element, Na (6)
15 Richer post (anag) — top administrative position in some universities and colleges (10)
19 Writer of words set to music (8)
20 Flower — girl's name (4)
21 Causing great distress (13)

DOWN

2 Strong negative reaction (8)
3 Edge (5)
4 Harmonious relationship (7)
5 Significance (5)
6 Very fashionable (2-5)
7 Edible ice cream container (4)
11 Trial performance for an artiste (8)
13 Before now (7)
14 Breed of terrier (7)
16 Ascent (5)
17 Self-satisfied smile (5)
18 Unit of (usually eight) bits (4)

Solution see page 282

199

ACROSS

1 US state, capital Madison (9)
8 Smell (5)
9 Attacked (3,4)
10 Miscellaneous (8)
11 Bony structure of the foot (4)
13 Not far away (6)
14 Saying it isn't so (6)
16 Look for (4)
17 Ask about (8)
19 Futile (7)
20 Normal (5)
21 Drop off (2,2,5)

DOWN

1 (Storage for) clothes (8)
2 Family member (6)
3 Palindromic man's name (4)
4 Disdainful (12)
5 Casually (12)
6 South African city (12)
7 Nobel stalled (anag) — boxing award (8,4)
12 Get plums (anag) — part of a wicket (3,5)
15 Struggle (6)
18 Precious stones (4)

Solution see page 282

200

ACROSS

1 Finished for ever (4,3,6)
8 Leguminous plant (4)
9 Head of a government department (8)
10 Number of those present (10)
12 Canadian province (6)
14 Provides what is required (6)
15 Rambling (10)
19 Painstakingly accurate (8)
20 Castle (4)
21 Skin specialist (13)

DOWN

2 Packed with incident (8)
3 Trip the light fantastic (5)
4 Itinerant (7)
5 West African country, formerly Dahomey (5)
6 Deference (7)
7 Paradise (4)
11 Foregoing (8)
13 Breach of social conventions (3,4)
14 Adviser (7)
16 Recce (5)
17 Body language of indifference (5)
18 Eat (4)

Solution see page 282

201

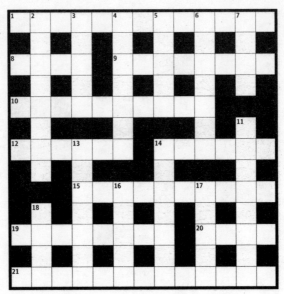

ACROSS

1 Substance aiding the production of suds (5,8)

8 Stopper (4)

9 Loose dressing gowns — paper coverings (8)

10 French school of painting and architecture of the 1880s (3,7)

12 Passage from the mouth to the stomach (6)

14 Celtic language (6)

15 Earlier (10)

19 What may go up when the rain comes down (8)

20 Without feeling (4)

21 Large herbivorous animal native to India, Nepal, Myanmar, Borneo and Sumatra (5,8)

DOWN

2 Fish–viewing tank (8)

3 Encourage (3,2)

4 Fine particles from cut wood (7)

5 Snow crystal (5)

6 Marry — take on as a cause (7)

7 Spanish currency unit (4)

11 Aromatic bark used as a spice (8)

13 Africa's oldest independent country (7)

14 Trash (7)

16 Erroneous (5)

17 Guess — sit with bad posture (5)

18 Christmas (4)

Solution see page 283

202

ACROSS

1 Help (6)
4 Unit of astronomical distance (6)
8 Small jazz band (5)
9 Downright (7)
10 Student (7)
11 Lustrous fabric (5)
12 Cathedral city in West Yorkshire (9)
17 More than enough (5)
19 Libidinous (7)
21 Accumulated (7)
22 Cereal (5)
23 Slipshod (6)
24 Walk wearily (6)

DOWN

1 Means of approach (6)
2 One way or another (7)
3 Mar (5)
5 Performer (7)
6 Small fish (5)
7 Shedding tears (6)
9 Calm (9)
13 Lively informal party (5-2)
14 Swindle (7)
15 Long-tailed parrots of Central and South America (6)
16 Dive (6)
18 Greek philosopher (5)
20 Cane or beet? (5)

Solution see page 283

203

ACROSS

1 Part of ear or leaf (4)
3 Medical fitness examination (8)
9 Travelling show with rides, games and much else (7)
10 Parts to play (5)
11 Lolly (5)
12 Invulnerable (6)
14 Capacity to cause trouble (8,5)
17 Hindu deity, the Preserver (6)
19 Error (5)
22 Natural stream (5)
23 He loots (anag) — southern African kingdom (7)
24 Separate (8)
25 Professional cook (4)

DOWN

1 Socialist (4-4)
2 Old West African kingdom from which 'bronze' sculptures were looted by the British in 1897 (5)
4 Poetic form used by Chaucer — ochre poultice (anag) (6,7)
5 Amber-coloured fluid in the blood (5)
6 Army officer ranking below a brigadier (7)
7 Carnal desire (4)
8 Fruit (for a split?) (6)
13 Full moon howler (8)
15 Hostile or cold nature (7)
16 Small travelling bag (6)
18 One on a long walk (5)
20 Sewn-on piece of material (5)
21 Move quickly (as if running before a gale) (4)

Solution see page 283

204

ACROSS

1 Well-padded sofa with two arms and a back (12)

9 Arm off a larger body of water between headlands (5)

10 The Seagull's author (7)

11 Agreeable — subtle (4)

12 Correct procedure (8)

14 SI base unit of thermodynamic temperature (6)

15 Conundrum (6)

18 Micro-organisms associated with food poisoning (8)

20 Powder (abbr) (4)

22 Weather map lines (7)

23 Dislike intensely (5)

24 Kind of scheme aimed at making fast bucks (3-4-5)

DOWN

2 Like the pattern on a snail's shell (7)

3 Fill totally (4)

4 Play it again! (6)

5 Brief (8)

6 Moral practice (5)

7 Cavalier (5-3-4)

8 Like David against Goliath? (5-7)

13 Well-educated readers (8)

16 Vivid — explicit (7)

17 Tasteless art (6)

19 Tobacco — hooter (5)

21 Capital of Azerbaijan (4)

Solution see page 283

205

ACROSS

1 Sausages' traditional partner (4)

3 Early spring flower (8)

8 Halt (4)

9 Part of a church at right angles to the nave (8)

11 Like double-barrelled names (or 'double-barrelled') (10)

14 Girl's name — colour (6)

15 Gratify (6)

17 Belligerence — hostility (10)

20 Freebie (8)

21 An Asian cuisine (4)

22 Document destroyer (8)

23 Margin (4)

DOWN

1 Highly desirable item (4-4)

2 Stinging arachnid (8)

4 Ordinary (6)

5 Strong desire to travel (10)

6 Vibrator in the mouthpiece of a wind instrument (4)

7 Youngest-ever British prime minister, d. 1806 (4)

10 Six states together making a region of the USA (3,7)

12 Disappeared (8)

13 Interim (8)

16 Covered walk with shops (6)

18 Eras (4)

19 State firmly (4)

Solution see page 284

206

ACROSS

1 Odious creep (10)

7 Uncommunicative (8)

8 Far from extreme (4)

9 Long-tailed bird of prey of the hawk family (4)

10 Throb (7)

12 Settle misunderstandings (5,3,3)

14 Nick a vehicle (7)

16 Strike violently (4)

19 Piece of foliage (4)

20 Oil from a citrus fruit used to flavour Earl Grey tea — to grab me (anag) (8)

21 Put your feet up (4,2,4)

DOWN

1 Follow stealthily (5)

2 Specially long and formal letter (7)

3 Top deity on Olympus (4)

4 Heated but petty argument (8)

5 Arboreal primate native to Madagascar (5)

6 Layer of roof slabs (6)

11 Melting pot (8)

12 Purplish-red (6)

13 22nd US state, joined 1819 (7)

15 Kind of orange (5)

17 Silly — ridiculous (5)

18 Legal document (4)

Solution see page 284

207

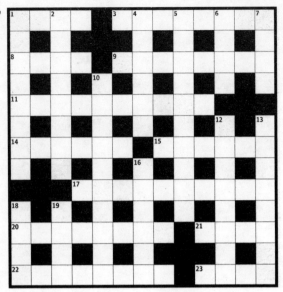

ACROSS

1 Silence! (4)

3 Tropical plant producing peppers — music cap (anag) (8)

8 Disdainful pout (4)

9 Ponder on (8)

11 Someone who looks very like another (4,6)

14 O, great! (anag) — a worthless fellow (6)

15 French fashion designer and perfumier, d. 1971 (6)

17 Having a resonant metallic sound (10)

20 Twig (6,2)

21 Rule Britannia's composer, d. 1778 (4)

22 Comic verse (8)

23 Pulses (4)

DOWN

1 Dampness (8)

2 Informer (what a swine!) (8)

4 Quantity (6)

5 Association of women linked by a common interest (10)

6 Yield (4)

7 Sort of brandy made from the remains of pressed grapes (4)

10 Burst forth (5,5)

12 Following the correct route (2,6)

13 Acts in a conceited way (8)

16 No longer fastened (6)

18 Sour to the taste (4)

19 For men only (4)

Solution see page 284

208

ACROSS

1 Cooked breakfast (stolen?) (7,3)
7 Portable anti-tank weapon (7)
8 Inhale audibly through the nose (5)
10 Jacob's twin brother (4)
11 High heel (8)
13 Not fair (6)
15 Associate socially with superiors (6)
17 Out of date (8)
18 Trademarked citrus fruit (4)
21 Stout pole with a foot rest — wading bird (5)
22 Noisy party (7)
23 Encourage departure from the straight and narrow? (4,6)

DOWN

1 Italian open pie (5)
2 Hailing call (4)
3 Fireside (6)
4 Refuse to accept (8)
5 Let sing (anag) — shine (7)
6 Fawning (10)
9 Over which one may walk (10)
12 Set apart (8)
14 Fair play (7)
16 State of inactivity (6)
19 Frivolous — liable to fall (5)
20 Landing stage (4)

Solution see page 284

209

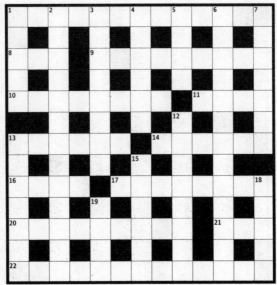

ACROSS

1 RAF officer (4,9)
8 Slack (3)
9 Capital of Gran Canaria (3,6)
10 Wholly (8)
11 Make woollen garments (4)
13 Second-largest country in the world by area (6)
14 Tribes (anag) — water-soluble brownish-yellow pigment (6)
16 Female singing voice (4)
17 Prediction (8)
20 Act independently (2,2,5)
21 Unwell (3)
22 Collection of photographs of known criminals (6,7)

DOWN

1 Author of The Picture of Dorian Gray (5)
2 Very little (4,2,7)
3 Boulder's state (8)
4 On the whole (6)
5 Absent (4)
6 Unrestrained in showing feelings (13)
7 Decoration made of ribbons (7)
12 Realised (anag) — relating to the stars (8)
13 Embarrassing blunder (with consequences that may reverberate) (7)
15 Goodbye (2,4)
18 Correspond (5)
19 Fierce wind (4)

Solution see page 285

210

ACROSS

1 Woman's shirt (6)

4 Noisy confusion of voices (5)

7 Line of fibres twisted to form a thread (6)

8 Rectangular array of mathematical data set out in rows and columns (6)

9 Desert of central China (4)

10 Division of an academic year (8)

12 Lather aiding beard removal (7,4)

17 With the press and public excluded (2,6)

19 One of a similar pair (4)

20 Armed robber (6)

21 Narcotic drug (6)

22 Herb used in cooking as seasoning (5)

23 Dash joining words (6)

DOWN

1 Baron Hardup's servant in Cinderella (7)

2 Egg-shaped wind instrument with finger holes (7)

3 Glancing blow (9)

4 Light-coloured marking on a horse's face (5)

5 Stiff cap worn by Roman Catholic clergy (7)

6 Extravagance (6)

11 Of birds that move seasonally (9)

13 Carriage for hire (7)

14 Largest living bird (7)

15 Wet (7)

16 Gallows (6)

18 Plant producing sweetcorn (5)

Solution see page 285

211

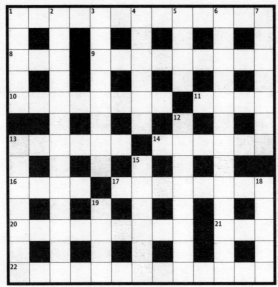

ACROSS

1 Chinese delicacy (5,4,4)

8 Raincoat (3)

9 Seizure of the levers of power (4,5)

10 Animal in its second 12   months (8)

11 Coagulated blood from a wound (4)

13 Useful device (6)

14 In the vicinity (6)

16 Female domestic servant (4)

17 Male official with a flag (8)

20 Moving from place to place (9)

21 Male feline (3)

22 Annual US horse race for threeyear- olds (8,5)

DOWN

1 Uneven (5)

2 Gearing that converts rotary to reciprocating motion (4-3-6)

3 Commonly designated (2-6)

4 Horse or donkey, perhaps (6)

5 Arranged neatly (4)

6 Portable boat engine (8,5)

7 Ceramic ware (7)

12 Down in the mouth (8)

13 Clever device to attract attention (7)

15 Take over by force (6)

18 Someone who objects to something being sited in their own locality (5)

19 South American country (4)

Solution see page 285

212

ACROSS

1 Poor handwriting (6)

4 Musical interval of 12 semitones (6)

8 Birthplace of the Prophet Mohammed (5)

9 Discordant (7)

10 Tiddly (7)

11 Heraldic device representing a family (5)

12 Coming from Taipei? (9)

17 Forelock brushed upward (5)

19 Red sauce (7)

21 Unpaid (7)

22 Holy Writ (5)

23 Thrill (6)

24 Storey (anag) (6)

DOWN

1 Triangular Indian turnover (6)

2 Narrate in detail (7)

3 Waterfront landing stage (5)

5 Small round boat of hides stretched over a wicker frame (7)

6 Existent (5)

7 The latest Henry or Edward? (6)

9 Careless pedestrian (9)

13 Vary the voice pitch (7)

14 Something shown in public (7)

15 Stick-in-the-mud — quadrangle (6)

16 Seem (6)

18 Father of Jacob and Esau (5)

20 Cat with a mottled coat (5)

Solution see page 285

213

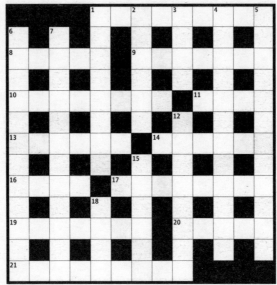

ACROSS

1 Build (9)

8 Drink the health of (5)

9 Well-defined abdominal muscles (3-4)

10 Woman's small handbag in the form of a pouch (8)

11 American composer of Three Places in New England, d. 1954 (4)

13 Endorsed (6)

14 Burn slightly (6)

16 Test (abbr) (4)

17 Reprimand firmly (8)

19 Judaism's Hell (7)

20 Sleep on (3,2)

21 Tough and uncompromising (4-5)

DOWN

1 Dead skin on fingernails (8)

2 Snuggle (6)

3 Send a written message by phone (4)

4 Taking place without being made public (12)

5 Acts on what is being implied (5,3,4)

6 Avoiding close contact (2,4,6)

7 Map-maker (12)

12 Trained (8)

15 Moral standards (6)

18 Name unknown (abbr) (4)

Solution see page 286

214

ACROSS

1 Excessively sentimental (10)
7 Left — late (8)
8 Small brook (4)
9 Put down (4)
10 Accelerate (5,2)
12 Without delay (2,3,6)
14 Hard-hearted (7)
16 First-class — fruit (4)
19 Engage by written agreement (4)
20 Good-natured (8)
21 Device to help breathing (10)

DOWN

1 Explosive projectile (5)
2 Two-wheeled horse-drawn vehicle used in battle (7)
3 Raps — successful recordings (4)
4 Assign to a new task (8)
5 Brass neck (5)
6 Refer to indirectly (6)
11 Childishly sulky (8)
12 Slow movement in a musical work (6)
13 Heavy material used to stabilise a ship (7)(5)
15 Sudden thrust in fencing (5)
17 Grinding tooth (5)
18 Plug (a gap) (4)

Solution see page 286

215

ACROSS

1 Essence (4)

3 Hot air — rich rote (anag) (8)

9 Annoyance (7)

10 Wanderer (5)

11 Instrument with stops (5)

12 Swelling on the big toe (6)

14 Relating to a country's representative abroad (13)

17 Electronic malfunction (6)

19 Object believed to have spiritual significance (5)

22 Dope (5)

23 Public school kid (7)

24 Person offering property to rent (8)

25 Friend (4)

DOWN

1 Of the chest (8)

2 Nasal sound (5)

4 Survive precariously (4,2,1,6)

5 North Italian city (5)

6 Pasta pillows (7)

7 Ringlet (4)

8 Seventh planet from the sun (6)

13 Leniency (8)

15 Gold and silver bars (7)

16 Choice (6)

18 All added together (5)

20 Fabric weave with parallel diagonal lines (5)

21 Factory (4)

Solution see page 286

216

ACROSS

1 Prostrate (4,9)
8 Overdue (7)
9 Wingless bloodsucker (5)
10 Short journey (4)
11 Cheeky (8)
13 Military aircraft (6)
14 Cell that conducts nerve impulses (6)
17 Making rigorous demands (8)
19 Fight verbally (4)
21 Declares (5)
22 City in Saxony, famous for its porcelain (7)
24 Come to a sudden and premature end (3,2,4,4)

DOWN

1 Chain for a pocket watch (3)
2 White metallic element found in most animals and plants, Ca (7)
3 Tiny circles (4)
4 Dilates (6)
5 Easy victory (8)
6 Established line of travel (5)
7 Bribe (informal) (9)
10 Plateau (9)
12 Throw overboard (8)
15 Quick witty reply (7)
16 Pin of a sundial whose shadow points to the hour (6)
18 Home (5)
20 Fail to meet — girl (4)
23 Open-meshed material (used for catching things?) (3)

Solution see page 286

217

ACROSS

1 Banter (8)
5 Not yet up (4)
9 Bestowed (5)
10 Agriculture (7)
11 Artistic district, part of the Left Bank in of Paris (12)
13 Kidney-shaped nut (6)
14 Go round — social group (6)
17 Lacking moral scruples (12)
20 Turbulent swift-flowing stream (7)
21 Tedium (5)
22 Barrel (4)
23 Shamefaced (8)

DOWN

1 Software problems (4)
2 Underhand — sneaky (7)
3 Knowing no more than before (4,3,5)
4 Belly laugh (6)
6 Great happiness (5)
7 Bad verse (8)
8 Illustration facing a book's title page (12)
12 Relating to sound (8)
15 City previously called Madras (7)
16 Prevent — frustrate (6)
18 Benefits (5)
19 Express a desire (upon a star?) (4)

Solution see page 287

218

ACROSS

1 Just (4)

3 Temporary structure around a building (8)

9 Blurt out (7)

10 Tactless remark (5)

11 Precipitation (5)

12 Position on a scale (6)

14 Involved in the most important part of a venture (2,3,5,3)

17 Cowardly (6)

19 Fire (5)

22 Foreign (5)

23 Push in (7)

24 Duplicitous (8)

25 Disease with a high death rate (4)

DOWN

1 In foreign parts (8)

2 Riches (5)

4 Grasp — knowledge (13)

5 Campaign against — quarrel (5)

6 Breach of the law (7)

7 Affair of honour (4)

8 Fortress (6)

13 Follower (8)

15 Discolour — sully (7)

16 (Musically) having a flexible tempo — our tab (anag) (6)

18 Poison (5)

20 Treat badly (5)

21 Oxen from Tibet (4)

Solution see page 287

219

ACROSS

1 Club used as a weapon (4)

3 Made an effort — put out (8)

8 Archaic exclamation of surprise (4)

9 Rubbish (8)

11 Choosy lads (anag) — life's learning time? (6,4)

14 Felt hat (6)

15 Dignified (6)

17 Social event for card players (5,5)

20 Flimsy carrier for one's purchases (5,3)

21 West African country (4)

22 Chatted (8)

23 Engrave (4)

DOWN

1 Oily liquid preservative — eco-store (anag) (8)

2 Blockbuster (5,3)

4 Exaggerate (6)

5 Stringed instrument played by turning a handle (5-5)

6 Portnoy's Complaint author, d. 2018 (4)

7 Spondulicks (4)

10 Toy — preoccupation (5,5)

12 Delighted (8)

13 Quite expensive (8)

16 Everything one owns — tea set (anag) (6)

18 Release (4)

19 Position (4)

Solution see page 287

220

ACROSS

1 $ (6,4)
7 Bright reddish-brown colour (5,3)
8 Top (4)
9 Key point (4)
10 District frequented by vagrants and addicts in America (4,3)
12 Done as a formality only (11)
14 Rugby position (3,4)
16 Cry like a child (4)
19 King of the jungle? (4)
20 Pirate's facial attire (8)
21 Cranky oldster (10)

DOWN

1 Architectural style of Ancient Greece (5)
2 Hard glossy coating (7)
3 Well ventilated (4)
4 Assistant to a more dominant person (informal) (8)
5 £1k (5)
6 Serious crime (6)
11 Bright headlight option (4,4)
12 Bony structure at the base of the spine (6)
13 Currently away from work (2,5)
15 Adherent of an eastern religion (5)
17 Dried or smoked pig meat (5)
18 Source — germ (4)

Solution see page 287

221

ACROSS

1 Basic (11)

9 Lackadaisical (9)

10 Pint glass of beer, perhaps (3)

11 Felony (5)

13 Twisting force (7)

14 Pulchritude (6)

15 Alleviation of pain or distress (6)

18 Baroque keyboard composition (7)

20 'Message received' (5)

21 Sphere (3)

22 Very complicated or detailed (9)

24 Instrument for registering earthquakes (11)

DOWN

2 Last month (abbr) (3)

3 Local language variation (7)

4 Powerful (6)

5 More pleasant (5)

6 Contiguous (9)

7 Popular 1920s' American dance (5,6)

8 Type of sausage (11)

12 Quick-tempered (9)

16 Previously (7)

17 Cuban leader, d. 2016 (6)

19 Assumed name (5)

23 Cleopatra's supposed nemesis (3)

Solution see page 288

222

ACROSS

1 Agricultural workers (9)
8 List of dishes (4)
9 Roast lamb condiment (4,5)
10 Courage and determination (4)
13 Evil presence (5)
15 What truants play? (6)
16 Black grape variety (6)
17 Illegal soft-nosed bullet (6)
19 Noun formed from a verb — nudger (anag) (6)
20 Eye's centre (5)
21 Something made with 16? (4)
24 Tenerife's main city (5,4)
25 Stretched circle? (4)
26 Soft toy (5,4)

DOWN

2 1936 alliance between Germany and Italy (4)
3 Nocturnal insect (4)
4 Lack of enthusiasm (6)
5 Authoritative declaration (6)
6 Crude oil (9)
7 Great number (9)
11 Spar with an imaginary opponent (6-3)
12 Body of legal rules based on custom and judicial precedent (6,3)
13 Rise (3,2)
14 Neither winning, nor losing (5)
18 Change into something else (6)
19 Adept — given (6)
22 Blackleg (4)
23 Brass wind instrument (4)

Solution see page 288

223

ACROSS

1 Appliance (6)

4 Trout-like fish found in mountain streams (5)

7 Period of instruction (6)

8 Superior in quality (2,4)

9 Thrombus (4)

10 Showing signs of stress and worry (8)

12 Disquiet (11)

17 Solidly built (8)

19 Small mountain lake (4)

20 Professional reviewer of literature, art, drama or music (6)

21 The Sunflower State (6)

22 Make off with (5)

23 Requiring speedy action (6)

DOWN

1 Think at length about (5,2)

2 Guest (7)

3 Aware of surroundings, sensations and thoughts (9)

4 Largest Greek island (5)

5 Watery (7)

6 Feeling regret (6)

11 One who courts danger on purpose (4-5)

13 Imposing building (7)

14 Friendly agreement between countries (7)

15 Taverns (anag) — retainer (7)

16 Old punishment device (6)

18 Small shrimp-like creatures eaten by whales (5)

Solution see page 288

224

ACROSS

1 Vehicular snarl-up (7,3)
7 Signal of dismissal (3,4)
8 Twisted (5)
10 Gusto (4)
11 Sorcery (5,3)
13 Capricious (6)
15 Light shoe (6)
17 Hairy-skinned fruit (informal) (8)
18 Revolve (4)
21 Edible entrails (5)
22 Group of digits on a US letter (3,4)
23 In total disorder (5-5)

DOWN

1 Rises and falls, nautically (5)
2 Strong drink distilled from fermented molasses (4)
3 5 down (6)
4 Very dark grey (8)
5 Blundering (7)
6 Unlicensed boxing match for money (10)
9 Killjoy (3,7)
12 Totally uninformed about what's going on (8)
14 Spicy Spanish pork sausage (7)
16 An appeal to the umpire? (6)
19 Person authorised to act for another (5)
20 Stout pole, nautically (4)

Solution see page 288

SOLUTIONS

1

BEFORELONG
UPINARMS AWAY
DUTY TRUANCY
COCOABUTTER
CASSOCK RICH
GLUE CONCEIVE
APOLOGETIC

2

ALBERT HASSLE
TYSON FAINTED
SPOONER BYRON
EFFICIENT
JOINKS OVATION
HOSPICE BASSO
ALLSET PRAYER

3

CUFF COMPARED
MOVE CIVILIAN
DIABOLICAL
WEALTH CENTRE
FAMILYTREE
UPGRADED LIAR
RESIDUAL OGLE

4

CUSTOM MUSSEL
ORBIT WEDLOCK
PARLOUS REPEL
AUDACIOUS
ARSON ASSUAGE
BARRACK TRILL
REMAKE ESCHEW

233

5

```
R E P O S E   O S C A R S
I   A   H       I   B   A
P O S S E   P O N T O O N
O   S   L   U   U   D   I
F E A R F U L   O V E R T
F   T     L   U         Y
  A P P R A I S A L
C     I     F     A     S
L I M B S   A M A L G A M
A   I   T   C   U   G   U
W I N S O M E   G U I L T
E   U   L       U   N   T
D E S I S T   G R O G G Y
```

6

```
L A D Y M U C K   B A S H
I   I   A   H   F   D   E
F L A I L   A M O R O U S
E   L   N   S   R   R   I
  B E L O W T H E B E L T
L   C   U   E   S       A
A R T E R Y   S H A M A N
S     I   C   A   A   T
H A R D S T A N D I N G
I   O   H   N   O   H   W
N E A T E S T   W A U G H
G   S   D   O   E   N   I
S E T H   C R E D I T O R
```

7

```
    G   D   C   S
  C O N S E C R A T E D
U   A   S   U   A   O
B R E W   C H E E R F U L
T     E   T   K   B
W A R N I N G   B E L L Y
I   U   T   C   R   E
I N D I A   H A S S O C K
C   S   C   N       R
C A T A R A C T   P O O R
L   N   D   A   L   S
  L A C E R A T I O N S
    E   E   A   T
```

8

```
C L O U D Y   B R E C H T
U   W   I   F   A   U   A
R U N O V E R   V E T C H
L   E   E   I   E   L   I
E R R O R   G A L L A N T
W       S   H       S   I
  A B S E N T E E I S M
E   A     E   X       A
U N C L E A N   A L D E R
C   A   L   I   M   E   R
L A R V A   N A P H T H A
I   D   T   G   L   E   N
D R I V E N   L E A R N T
```

234

```
H I S T O R Y I S B U N K
I   A   B   A   P   N   A
P A L   T A P D A N C E R
O   T   R   P   M   E   A
O V E R U S E D   C R O C
  D   D   R   S   E   H
Y I P P E E   S C A M P I
A   E   D   B   E   O
S H A H   E A R N I N G S
H   N   Y   D   A   I   A
M O U S E D E E R   O W L
A   T   T   G   I   U   O
K I S S I N G C O U S I N
```

```
W I T T I C I S M   S   B
  B   I   A   K   B O A R
B I R D B R A I N   B   I
  S   E   D   B   B R E D
I   S   B I G O T   I   L
S E C U R E   B I S Q U E
O   O   A       G   U   W
S T R E S S   B O D E G A
C   P   S P U R N   T   Y
E M I T   R   O   T   J
L   O   H I L A R I O U S
E R N E   N   C   F   T
S   S   I T C H Y F E E T
```

```
A B S T I N E N T   L   H
  U   E   Y   U   C O S Y
A S T R O L O G Y   V   B
  H   M   O   G   S E E R
B   P   S N E E R   M   I
A G E N T S   T A B A R D
N   R   E       N   T   C
D E F E A T   F U L C R A
O   O   M I X U P   H   R
L O R D   L   L   P   S
E   A   I L L H E A L T H
R I T Z   E   A   W   U
O   E   P R O M I N E N T
```

```
S A F E T Y C U R T A I N
W   I   R   A   E   M   U
I A N   E X C H E Q U E R
S   N   K   H   K   S   S
S P A R K L E R   G E N E
    N   I   T   N   M   R
T A H I N I   N A M E L Y
E   A   G   S   G   N
M O D E   S T E A L T H Y
P   D   P   R   S   P   U
E S O T E R I C A   A I M
S   C   S   F   K   R   M
T A K E T H E M I C K E Y
```

SOLUTIONS

13

```
C A S U A L   S P U R N S
A   E   T     I   A     T
R O D E O   F A R R I E R
E   U   L   O   A   D   O
S E C U L A R   E A S E L
S   E   G   U         L
    D I S P E N S E R
B     A   T       O   A
U R B A N   F A S H I O N
R   U   G   U   A   S   N
I M M O R A L   T I T L E
E   P   I       I   E   A
D I S M A L   P E T R O L
```

14

```
P O S E   S W I T C H O N
A   Q     H   A   E   O
R O U E   D I P L O M A T
A   E   A   N   K   P   E
G R E E D Y G U T S
U   G   J   E   U   I   R
A V E N U E   G R U N G E
Y   E   D   F   K   V   A
    M I N U T E H A N D
S   I   C   R   Y   S   Y
L A B R A D O R   F I R M
A   I   T   R       O   I
B E S I E G E D   O N Y X
```

15

```
B R E A S T T H E T A P E
A   I   C   H   G   G   P
T U G   A S R E G A R D S
O   H   N   I   S   E   I
N O T A T A L L   H E A L
    S   I   L   C   T   O
T O O T E D   D I S O W N
O   M   S   U   N   D
W E E K   I N D E N I A L
P   R   L   W   A   F   A
A M E N I T I E S   F U N
T   E   M   N   T   E   K
H A L E A N D H E A R T Y
```

16

```
  S T R O N G H O L D
  T   E   A   O   U   T
S U C C I N C T   N E A R
  M   L   A   L   D   N
P O U T   T I D Y I N G
    S   I   N       E
G R E E N K E E P E R
A     F   S   U
W R E S T L E   B R I G
N   E   A   B   P   E
H E A P   T E A T O W E L
  T   I   E   R   S   S
  J A R D I N I E R E
```

17

18

19

20

SOLUTIONS

21

	P	U	E	R	T	O	R	I	C	O	
P	E		A	U		O		A			
A	C	C	U	S	E	R		S	P	R	E	E
C	A		T		G		E		T		A
K	E	N	T		F	I	L	M	N	O	I	R
A			G		D		A		O		T
N	E	C	T	A	R		B	R	U	N	C	H
I		A		R	S		Y				Q
M	A	L	I	G	N	E	D		T	H	O	U
A	Y		O		R	A		A	A	A
L	I	P	P	Y		M	U	B	A	R	A	K
	S		L		O		E		R		E
	H	O	M	E	A	N	D	D	R	Y	

22

D	R	E	S	S	E	R		C		C		R
A		R		P		I	S	O	L	A	T	E
C	A	R	D	I	A	C		N		R		C
H		O		L		T	E	S	T	A	T	E
A	P	R	I	L		U		C		F		S
	A		T		T	E	S	T	I	N	E	S	S
	T		H		E		E		T		I
C	H	A	M	E	L	E	O	N		I	
O		B		B		N		T	W	E	R	P
P	E	R	V	E	R	T		I		R		U
P		U		A		R	I	O	T	O	U	S
E	X	P	E	N	S	E		U		D		A
R		T		S		E	P	S	T	E	I	N

23

A	D	D	I	C	T		C	A	L	V	E	S
L		I		R		L		C		A		H
L	A	C	T	O	S	E		H	O	M	E	R
U		E		E		T		E		P		I
R	I	D	E	S		O	L	D	N	I	C	K
E			U		F			R		R	E
	C	R	E	S	T	F	A	L	L	E	N
D		E			S		O				M
R	E	D	O	U	B	T		C	O	R	G	I
A		R		N		E		K		U		D
W	H	E	A	T		A	B	J	U	R	E	D
E		S		I		M		A		A		L
R	U	S	H	E	D		T	W	E	L	V	E

24

	F	R	A	G	M	E	N	T	A	R	Y	
T		U		E		D		A		E		B
E	X	T	E	N	S	I	O	N		E	W	E
S			E		B		G		E	X		N
T	A	S	E	R		L	E	O	P	A	R	D
I		A		I		E			M		T
M	I	M	I	C	S		G	A	R	I	S	H
O		A			W		N		N		E
N	A	R	R	A	T	E		S	L	E	E	K
I		I		B		E		W			N
A	C	T		I	M	P	R	E	C	A	T	E
L		A		D		I		R		I		E
	U	N	N	E	C	E	S	S	A	R	Y	

25

26

27

28

SOLUTIONS

29

30

31

32

33

```
M A N O F T H E W O R L D
O   E   A   O   O   E   E
W R E C K E R   N E A R S
    D   E   A   D   C   E
A L L Y   S C O R C H E R
B   E   H   E   O       T
S O D D E N   L U M B E R
O   L   E   S   E       A
R A M B L I N G   B R A T
B   I   B   R   H   G
E R N I E   A N A E M I A
N   S   N   G   I   A   X
T A K E T H E P L U N G E
```

34

```
        J   U   T   C
      R O U N D H E A D   D
    V   I   I   R   R   F
C A I N   Q U A N D A R Y
N   E   U   S       E
F I D D L E   H I G H E R
S   I       A   S
T H A N K S   S A N C H O
I   A   T   G   E
S N A C K B A R   L E E R
  G   U   R   I   I
    S T R E T C H E D
    E   S   T   R
```

35

```
A S S E T S T R I P P E R
N   H   I   A   T   A   E
G O A   M O U S E T R A P
E   R   I   N   M   A   U
R A P I D I T Y   O P A L
    P   I   S   I   H   S
C U R A T E   I N H E R E
O   A   Y   D   A   R
R A C E   C O N F I N E D
N   T   F   M   L   A   W
C H I P O L A T A   L I E
O   C   R   I   S   I   L
B L E E D I N G H E A R T
```

36

```
  C O M P R E H E N D E D
E   N   O   F   T   R   O
F U G U E   F I R E A R M
F   O   T   O   U   P   E
E R I E   B R U S S E L S
R   N   T   T   C   D
V A G A R Y   M A N T R A
E   A   D   N   E   Y
S E A S N A I L   S N U B
C   S   Q   R   S   D   O
E X C L U D E   C A R G O
N   O   I   C   U   I   K
T I T T L E T A T T L E
```

SOLUTIONS

37

G	O	B	B	L	E		B	R	I	B	E	S
O		U		U		S		O		A		H
A	T	T	E	M	P	T		D	E	C	O	R
W		C		P		I		I		C		I
A	C	H	E	S		F	U	N	C	H	A	L
Y				U		F				I		L
	C	O	M	M	O	N	P	L	A	C	E	
P		Y		E		E		E				B
A	R	S	E	N	I	C		G	O	R	G	E
S		T		O		K		I		O		H
C	H	E	E	R		E	M	B	R	A	C	E
A		R		S		D		L		L		L
L	A	S	T	E	D		W	E	D	D	E	D

38

	C	O	N	T	R	A	D	I	C	T	
A		H		A		E		Y		O	
C	R	A	M	P	O	N		S	Y	N	O	D
C		I		E		T		L		T		I
R	A	N	K		C	A	R	E	L	E	S	S
E				F		L		X		N		O
D	R	A	G	O	N		B	I	N	D	E	R
I		R		R		J		A				D
T	A	S	T	E	F	U	L		B	O	R	E
E		E		S		D		H		W		R
D	E	N	S	E		G	R	A	P	N	E	L
		A		E		E		R		E		Y
	B	L	I	N	D	S	I	D	E	D	

39

	B	E	T	W	E	E	N	T	I	M	E	S
T		M		A		X		E		O		O
A	M	B	I	T		T	U	R	M	O	I	L
K		R		T		E		M		S		I
E	Y	O	T		I	N	D	I	G	E	N	T
T		I		B		D		N				A
H	E	L	M	E	T		G	A	S	P	E	R
E				Q		V		L		R		I
W	E	L	L	U	S	E	D		A	E	O	N
H		I		E		N		B		T		E
E	N	G	L	A	N	D		U	S	E	R	S
E		H		T		E		S		N		S
L	A	T	C	H	K	E	Y	K	I	D	S	

40

	B	O	T	H	E	R	S	O	M	E	
A		R		I		X		L		O	
B	L	O	W	N	U	P		I	N	D	I	A
S		W		Y		I		P		E		L
T	O	N	S		P	R	O	P	O	S	A	L
E				D		E		E		T		K
M	I	D	D	A	Y		C	R	A	Y	O	N
I		E		E		S		S				O
O	V	E	R	D	R	A	W		A	V	O	W
U		P		A		L		P		A		I
S	I	S	A	L		M	O	U	F	L	O	N
		E		U		O		N		U		G
	M	A	I	S	O	N	E	T	T	E	

41

42

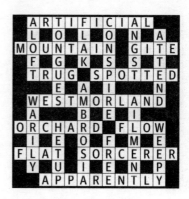

43

44

SOLUTIONS

45

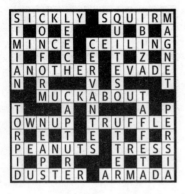

46

47

48

49

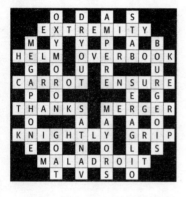

50

51

52

SOLUTIONS

53

54

55

56

57

H	O	B	O		W	O	O	D	L	A	N	D
A		I		S		V		E		D		A
B	E	G	U	I	L	E		V	I	V	I	D
I		H		M		R		I		A		O
T	A	T	U	M		S	P	L	I	N	T	
U				E		T				C		S
A	L	T	E	R	N	A	T	I	V	E	L	Y
L		H		T				N		N		N
	C	O	F	F	E	E		V	A	S	C	O
U		R		I		M		A		P		N
S	H	I	F	T		E	L	D	E	R	L	Y
E		U		I		N		E		E		M
R	U	M	I	N	A	T	E		V	E	T	S

58

	A	S	S	E	S	S		H	I	L	L	S
	R		P		H			A		E		C
E	C	L	A	I	R		B	I	S	T	R	O
	H		R		U		K		D			U
W	A	I	T		B	I	B	U	L	O	U	S
	I		A		B		I			W		E
	C	O	N	C	E	A	L	M	E	N	T	
C		P		R		A		N		O		
A	M	E	T	H	Y	S	T		R	I	T	E
U		N		O		E		A		T		
S	T	A	P	L	E		R	E	G	R	E	T
E		I		L			A		E		R	
S	U	R	L	Y		G	L	A	D	L	Y	

59

T	O	M	T	H	U	M	B		R	I	F	T
A		A		I		O		H		D		A
A	R	O	M	A	N		H	O	O	D	L	U	M
T		M		D		A		R		E		A
	C	O	N	Q	U	I	S	T	A	D	O	R
B		T		U		R		I				I
R	E	H	E	A	T		A	C	U	M	E	N
O				R		V		U		A		D
W	A	L	K	T	H	E	P	L	A	N	K	
B		A		E		R		T		H		P
E	A	R	D	R	U	M		U	S	U	A	L
A		V		S		I		R		N		A
T	E	A	L		A	N	C	E	S	T	R	Y

60

	C	O	N	U	R	B	A	T	I	O	N	
A		W		N		I		H		B		G
D	O	N	T	A	S	K	M	E		J	A	R
O				I		I		F		E		A
L	U	C	I	D		N	O	T	I	C	E	S
E		H		E		I				T		S
S	H	A	R	D	S		V	A	N	I	S	H
C		M		K		N		V				O
E	X	P	L	O	D	E		C	H	E	A	P
N		A		R		N		I				P
T	A	G		I	V	Y	L	E	A	G	U	E
S		N		E		A		N		E		R
	W	E	L	L	I	N	G	T	O	N	S	

SOLUTIONS

61

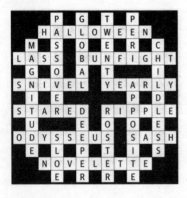

62

63

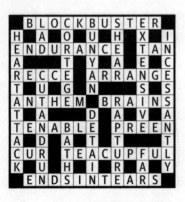

64

65

```
P I G E O N H O L E
A   A   R   A   A S
O V E R C A S T   P I T H
  E   M   L   T   S   R
  D E E P   F R E E D O M
  N   P   I       N
  G E T C R A C K I N G
  R   O   K   N
B O R S C H T   S H U T
  W   W   I   M   U   W
P U M A   B R U M M I E S
  P   Z   I   L   A   E
  T I E T H E K N O T
```

66

```
B U R S A R   F L A B B Y
U   U   T   C   A   O   E
C E D I L L A   P A N T S
K   D   A   L   A   A   S
L A Y E R   L O Z E N G E
E   E   G   T   Z   S
  C O M E W H A T M A Y
S   S   E   H   A
T I M E O U T   R I D E R
R   O   R   U   O   R   C
A T S E A   N O U R I S H
T   I   T   E   G   V   L
A N S W E R   C H E E S Y
```

67

```
  K   R   P   S
A M E L I O R A T E D
  D   R   S   O   A   I
B U L B   S L U G G I S H
  L   O   D   N   H
S T I F F L Y   W A L T Z
  E   O   E   N   N   H
P R A N G   F E A T H E R
  A   D   B   P   D
S T A N D O U T   B O I L
  E   E   R   U   E   R
  D I S C E R N M E N T
  S   D   E   F
```

68

```
B O D Y   E P I D E M I C
I   I   R   E   E   L
D U S K   B E L G R A D E
D   S   B   A   E   D   F
A D O L E S C E N T
B   L   A   H   E   D   A
L I V E R Y   O R D E A L
E   E   G   D   A   T   D
    B A L U S T R A D E
S   K   R   R   E   C   R
A B E R D E E N   S H I N
C   E   E   S   E   E   E
K I N D N E S S   E D G Y
```

SOLUTIONS

69

70

71

72

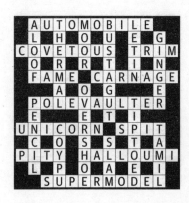

73

Row 1: EXCRUCIATING
Row 2: D F O O C N L
Row 3: REALM NACELLE
Row 4: O C P V E E N
Row 5: PETS DESPOTIC
Row 6: A O H X T A
Row 7: CARBON SELDOM
Row 8: L R B D E P
Row 9: ASSASSIN BLAB
Row 10: N T E O M I E
Row 11: GROMMET ANVIL
Row 12: E R E I N E L
Row 13: REMANDCENTRE

74

Row 1: BELTANDBRACES
Row 2: I E C A E R E
Row 3: TRACTOR GRASP
Row 4: V S W I W A
Row 5: BEER CIRCULAR
Row 6: E R L N I A
Row 7: EUSTON ADROIT
Row 8: L T U E N E
Row 9: ZUCCHINI RAND
Row 10: E H A E D R
Row 11: BLAIR SEADOGS
Row 12: U R I C N L A
Row 13: BUTTONONESLIP

75

Row 1: GASTRONOMY
Row 2: D U L A A A
Row 3: ELEGIAC RANCH
Row 4: C S P I C S O
Row 5: LAST SNOOTIER
Row 6: U D G S O O
Row 7: TESTER DIRNDL
Row 8: T P V C S O
Row 9: EPILOGUE AGOG
Row 10: R N T R W R I
Row 11: SWAMI DEALERS
Row 12: C O L I E T
Row 13: CHANCELLOR

76

Row 1: COPENHAGEN
Row 2: O A O U V A
Row 3: PRONOUNS OUZO
Row 4: O A S T K O
Row 5: TICK ARREARS
Row 6: H B I E
Row 7: BUENOSAIRES
Row 8: A A N A
Row 9: ENDLESS WINO
Row 10: G O T M M N
Row 11: HEAD FRENETIC
Row 12: R G U A N O
Row 13: WELLINGTON

SOLUTIONS

77

Across solutions include: HAILESELASSIE, MAD, DROPSCONE, DISINTER, HERA, HOOKER, ALCOTT, TOIL, ZEPPELIN, EDITORIAL, TIN, KINDREDSPIRIT

78

Across solutions include: POLLSTER, THUD, ROGUE, GRANITE, CLARINETTIST, ORPHAN, ONEOFF, INPERPETUITY, FILBERT, HYPER, REAP, NEUROSIS

79

Across solutions include: TYMPANUM, PANG, MOGUL, BAHRAIN, CANTANKEROUS, UTTERS, SEDATE, BRONTOSAURUS, OUTDOOR, GRIMY, KICK, HYDROGEN

80

Across solutions include: DELIBERATE, GAUNTLET, TACO, ONUS, BLUNDER, CIRCUMSPECT, SPINDLY, BIAS, MOOR, TAKEHOLD, REINSTATED

81

```
F E A T   S P O R A D I C
A   N   I   U   A   E   O
L O G I C A L   B E A N O
L   E   E   L   A   R   P
F O R U M   E S T H E R
L   A   D   S       B
A D M I N I S T R A T O R
T   E   T   E       U
  B A N G E R   S U S A N
C   N   L   I   I   A   E
H E D G E   N O D O U B T
A   E   A   G   E   N   T
D A R K N E S S   W A K E
```

82

```
E R S A T Z   S H A D E S
X   T   R       U   R   E
T H E M E   B A R R A G E
R   W   N   E   D   I   T
A L A D D I N   L Y N C H
S   R   C   E       E
  D A R K H O R S E
S   U   M       N   B
T A P A S   A C C U S A L
A   E   T   R   A   N   I
L E R W I C K   B E A S T
E   I   C   E   R   H
R E L I S H   F R E E Z E
```

83

```
  A P H R O D I S I A C
O   E   O   R   H   B   D
K O A L A B E A R   S K I
T   S   A   E   T   S
O N S E T   M A W K I S H
B   U   E   Y   N   T
E X P O R T   A F R E S H
R   R   G   O   N   E
F R E E S I A   G A T E D
E   M   N   N   L   I
S P A   O L D M A S T E R
T   C   R   E   M   E   T
  M Y S T E R Y P L A Y
```

84

```
S T R A I G H T F A C E D
T   E   M   A   E   O   E
I M P   P I M P E R N E L
C   R   R   M   S   T   A
K E E L O V E R   N A V Y
    H   V   R   T   C   E
E L E V E N   R E S T E D
L   N   D   G   A   L
E R S E   D O S S I E R S
G   I   C   B   P   N   T
I M B R O G L I O   S O U
A   L   U   I   O   E   D
C H E A P A N D N A S T Y
```

SOLUTIONS

85

86

87

88

89

```
Y E L L O W F L A G
 E   E K   O     S     R
K A N G A R O O     K I E V
 S   W   A     T   E     T
 T R O Y     S H O W B I Z
     R   A   O           N
 B A K E D A L A S K A
 U     R   D   U
I N E R T I A   C L U B
 G   A   A   K   T     E
 S L O B   T E E N A G E R
 E   B   I   E   N     F
   M I S C E L L A N Y
```

90

```
S H I P W R E C K     R     B
   I   O   O     A   P I E R
V E S T I B U L E     G     E
   D   S   R   A   W H O A
G   S   M O V I E     T     T
L A C K E Y     S Q U A S H
A   A   D       U   W     E
D E T R O P   S A L A M I
I   T   C R U E L   Y     N
A X E D   O   V   T   O
T   R   B L U E P R I N T
O V E R   I   R   O   U
R   D   E X P E R T I S E
```

91

```
W I D E O F T H E M A R K
O   I   P   O   M   R   I
N O S   P T A R M I G A N
G   E   O   M   A   U   D
A M N E S I A C   E M I R
    G   I   N   H   E   E
R E A C T S   P E R N O D
O   G   E   P   L   T
O W E N   K I N S H A S A
F   M   H   L   I   T   U
T H E N A G A I N   I A N
O   N   Z   F   K   V   T
P E T T Y O F F I C E R S
```

92

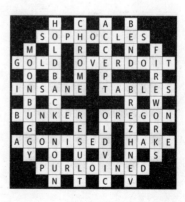

```
     H   C   A   B
   S O P H O C L E S
 M   L   R   C   N   F
G O L D   O V E R D O I T
O   B   M   P       R
I N S A N E   T A B L E S
B   C       R   W
B U N K E R   O R E G O N
G       E   L   Z   R
A G O N I S E D   H A K E
Y   O   U   V   N   S
   P U R L O I N E D
     N   T   C   V
```

SOLUTIONS

93

94

95

96

97

```
. G O B S T O P P E R .
A . E . O . A . X . . .
S U C C U M B . T E H E E
S . K . E . O . H . A . N
I V O R . C O V E R L E T
S . . C . T . T . E . . H
T O U C H Y . C I N D E R
A . N . O . C . C . . . A
N O T I O N A L . M A L L
T . R . C . X . C . M . L
S O U T H . T U R B I N E
. . T . O . O . O . T . D
. T H R O W N A W A Y .
```

98

```
. . . A T T H E M O S T
A . B . R . A . T . U . R
M E E T S . M A N A T E E
P . N . O . E . A . M . A
H E D O N I S T . D A I S
E . S . I . T . S . N . U
T H I R S T . D E T O U R
A . N . T . C . A . E . E
M A I M . T H O R O U G H
I . S . M . U . C . V . U
N I T P I C K . H E R O N
E . E . K . M . E . T
S H R I N K A G E
```

99

```
. D O N O T D I S T U R B
S . R . E . A . P . E
W A R T Y . C O U N S E L
E . S . X . A . C . E . O
E M M Y . U N D E R T O W
T . A . C . T . P . . . T
W A N T O N . H A U N C H
I . . L . G . N . I . . E
L A W C O U R T . D R U B
L . H . R . O . D . V . E
I N E X A C T . E M A I L
A . A . D . T . L . N . T
M E T R O P O L I T A N
```

100

```
B L O S S O M . C . H . O
O . W . A . A M O R O U S
W I N D B A G . N . R . T
L . E . R . N O S T R I L
S C R E E . U . C . I . E
. O . . R E M A I N D E R
. H . A . . E . . . A
G O B E T W E E N . . S
U . E . T . A . T E S T S
I N S U L T S . I . A . T
T . I . I . T R O L L E Y
A L D E N T E . U . V . E
R . E . G . R A S H E R S
```

SOLUTIONS

101

102

103

104

105

```
A U D I T O R   C   A   M
D   E   H   A J A C C I O
D A N G E R S   T   C   L
E   E   G   C H E R O O T
D E B A R   A   G   S   E
  Z     I L L G O T T E N
  R   M     R       R   O
P A P A R A Z Z I     R
I   E   E   E   C R O S S
S U N L A M P   A   M   O
T   P   P   H O L D A L L
I M A G E R Y   L   H   I
L   L   R   R E Y N A R D
```

106

```
S T A T E O F T H E A R T
  O   I   R   A   X   E
S M O G   D E C I P H E R
W   H   E   I   R   D
M O N T M A R T R E S
L   L   L     S   D
A F T E R S   P A S T E L
  E   N     O       C
      D E P I L A T O R Y
  H   U   A   E   O   E
T A R R A G O N   M O A T
  L   E   A   T   E   S
G O L D E N H A M S T E R
```

107

```
B L O B B Y   I N K P O T
E   N   U   D   U   I   R
F R A Z Z L E   D I Z Z Y
O   I   Z   V   G   A   I
G A R D A   O V E R R U N
S     R   L       R   G
  V L A D I V O S T O K
U   I   E   C       B
T A N T R U M   R A D I I
O   C   H   E   A   R   O
P U T T Y   N E W M O O N
I   U   M   T   N   O   I
A N S W E R   C Y C L I C
```

108

```
B L I N D M A N S B U F F
  E   Y   E   A   A   A
E T A L   S U I T C A S E
  L   O   S   V   K   T
D O W N A T H E E L
  O       I       O   A
A S T E R N   P A G O D A
  E   P     R       H
    I L L F O U N D E D
  G   T   E   C   I   S
C A R A P A C E   G L I B
  G   P   R   S   H   O
A S T H I N G S S T A N D
```

SOLUTIONS

109

110

111

112

113

C	O	N	S	E	C	U	T	I	V	E	L	Y
	F		W		A		I		I		O	
A	C	M	E		P	E	D	I	C	U	R	E
O		L		A		A		T		E		
H	U	L	L	A	B	A	L	O	O			
R		I		L				R		B		
E	S	C	A	P	E		S	I	S	K	I	N
E		I		U				U		N		
	D		M	O	D	E	R	A	T	E	L	Y
	D		L		U		P		E		A	
M	A	T	E	R	N	A	L		N	U	D	E
	W		S		N		U		O		E	
O	N	A	S	H	O	E	S	T	R	I	N	G

114

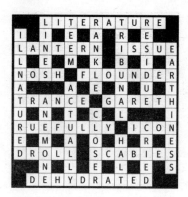

	L	I	T	E	R	A	T	U	R	E	
I		I		E		A		R		E	
L	A	N	T	E	R	N		I	S	S	U	E
L		E		M		K		B		I		A
N	O	S	H		F	L	O	U	N	D	E	R
A			A		E		N		U		T
T	R	A	N	C	E		G	A	R	E	T	H
U		N		T		C		L			I
R	U	E	F	U	L	L	Y		I	C	O	N
E		M		A		O		H		R		E
D	R	O	L	L		S	C	A	B	I	E	S
		N		L		E		L		E		S
	D	E	H	Y	D	R	A	T	E	D	

115

		C		B		A		O		
	M	A	N	O	E	U	V	R	E	
	L		T		G		G		A		I
B	O	L	T		A	Q	U	A	L	U	N	G
S		I		R		S			R	
R	E	V	E	R	T		T	A	I	L	E	D
H		S				N		A	
F	E	T	T	L	E		B	A	F	F	L	E
A			A		B	U		I	
P	R	O	C	U	R	E	R		S	I	T	S
T		H		W		A		I		Y
	D	E	P	I	C	T	I	O	N	
		W		G		E		N		

116

			C	O	U	G	H	D	R	O	P
V		L		U		P		O		E		R
A	R	I	E	L		B	R	O	C	A	D	E
N		V		P		E		P		L		D
T	R	I	M	A	R	A	N		K	I	W	I
A		N		B		T		O		T		L
G	I	G	O	L	O		G	R	O	Y	N	E
E		S		E		B		A		C		C
P	A	T	H		C	R	O	T	C	H	E	T
O		A		C		E		O		E		I
I	N	T	E	R	I	M		R	E	C	T	O
N		U		E		E		I		K		N
T	A	E	K	W	O	N	D	O	

SOLUTIONS

117

```
    E C S B
  A F G H A N H O U N D
  V   G   L   O   D   E
S O N S   L A U D A B L E
  I       E   T   P   E
P R O C U R E   D E A T H
  D   O   S   Q   S   E
F U N N Y   M U S T A R D
  P   T   H   I   I
H O M E R U L E   G L O W
  I   M   R   T   O   U
  S U P E R F L U O U S
    T   Y   Y   N
```

118

```
    O N O N E S F E E T
E   A   B   N   L   X
N E S T E G G   A L P H A
D   I   Y   U   G   U   S
E L S E   C L A R I N E T
A     I   F   A   G   O
R E F I N E   I N T E R N
M   R   F   S   T     I
E M I N E N C E   B A T S
N   G   R   H   R   H
T R A I N   A T I S S U E
    T   A   P   N   O   D
  H E L L B E N T O N
```

119

```
  U N C H A R I T A B L E
H   A   O   E   A   E   A
E X I T S   S N I G G E R
A   R   T   E   L   E   D
R I O T   A N I S E T T E
T   B   C   T   P     F
E D I T O R   T I N G L E
L   L   A   N   R   N
L A D Y L O V E   B E A D
T   R   U   E   H   A   E
H O A R D E R   A C T O R
A   K   E   S   R   E   S
T R E N D S E T T E R S
```

120

```
A T T H E S A M E T I M E
R   A   O   A   A     O
L I M B   C A G L I A R I
F   I   K   M   L     E
A L L T H E R A G E
I       Y       N   P
E N T R E E   M A D C A P
G   E       A       R
    D I S T R I B U T E
  C   M   M   T   I   I
H U M I L I T Y   L A C E
  B   S   T   R   L   L
B E A T T H E S Y S T E M
```

121

```
A T T R A C T E D . M . F
. U . U . A . N . B O A R
G R A T I T U D E . R . U
. F . H . C . U . S T A G
S . A . C H A R M . I . A
C O M E L Y . E Y E F U L
U . B . O . . R . I . I
L O U N G E . A R D E N T
P . L . S L A S H . D . Y
T H A W . D . S . U . J
U . N . A E G E A N S E A
R A C Y . S . N . I . E
E . E . S T A T U T O R Y
```

122

```
. A G H A S T . F E W E R
. P . E . U . E . I . E
A P P L E S . F I L L I P
. L . P . T . N . I . E
C A L F . A N A T H E M A
. U . U . I . M . S . L
. D E L I N Q U E N T S .
W . X . E . S . E . H .
A T T E N D E E . G O Y A
R . R . O . M . L . N
M E A G R E . E X E T E R
T . C . T . N . C . S
H I T C H . S T A T U S
```

123

```
. . P A C K H O R S E
P . R . A . O . U . I . N
E X U L T . D E F I C I T
D . N . H . D . F . H . O
A B O V E A L L . C A L M
L . F . T . E . S . R . O
P A T O I S . V A N D A L
U . H . C . P . N . N . O
S L E W . C O A S T I N G
H . M . A . T . K . X . I
E R I T R E A . R O O K S
R . L . E . T . I . N . T
S P L A S H O U T
```

124

```
C U S T A R D P O W D E R
O . M . N . U . S . E . E
G L I T T E R . S O N I C
. . T . E . H . I . S . U
B I T E . H A L F T E R M
Y . E . V . M . I . . . B
Z O N K E D . S E V E R E
A . . N . E . D . M . N
N O S E D I V E . S P I T
T . T . E . A . H . T
I N E R T . D I A R I S T
U . P . T . E . L . E . A
M U S T A R D P O W D E R
```

SOLUTIONS

125

```
  J A C K S O N V I L L E
G   B   I   L   I   I   A
A S Y E T   D E N O T E S
M   S   H   M   D   H   Y
E M M Y   J A L A P E N O
S   A   A   N   L       N
M E L O D Y   H O B B I T
A   V   P   O   L       H
N E W C O M E R   P U C E
S   A   C   A   Y   B   E
H O G W A S H   O H B O Y
I   O   A   E   G   E   E
P E N I T E N T I A R Y
```

126

```
      L   C   K   H
  S H E N A N I G A N S
  A   A   R   T   Y   W
A V I D   D E T E S T E D
O       I   Y   T   E
G I R A F F E   F A I N T
R   D   F   B   C   E
O F F E R   J O C K E Y S
A   Q   L   G       T
D I S U N I T Y   M O O S
R   A   T   M   A   D
E N T E R T A I N E D
  E   E   N   Y
```

127

```
  B U D G I E   M A C H O
  A   I   N   I   H   O
B Y W O R D   E X P A N D
  L   R   E   E   S   L
B E T A   L A C R O S S E
  A   M   I   E   I   S
  F L A B B E R G A S T
A   E   L   T   N   A
V U V U Z E L A   D U C K
A   E   L   I   O   T
T U R N O N   N O R D I C
A   E   T   L   R   L
R A T T Y   G Y R A T E
```

128

```
C Y C L O P S   T   A   U
A   L   N   E C H E L O N
M E E K E S T   R   M   V
E   A   I   T H E R O P E
L E N I N   L   E   S   I
  A   A N E C D O T A L
  C   M       A       R
C H E M I S T R Y       N
U   X   L   A   E X T O L
C A T A L A N   V   W   I
K   A   I   G E E G E E S
O W N G O A L   N   E   L
O   T   N   E N T I T L E
```

129

130

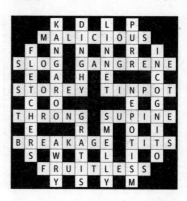

131

132

SOLUTIONS

133

```
F I G H T O R F L I G H T
. N . A . B . L . N . U .
O D D S . S H O C K I N G
. I . T . C . R . W . S .
A C C E L E R A T E . . .
. A . . . N . . . L . A .
S T R O V E . S O L E M N
. E . F . . . W . . . B .
. . F A L L A C I O U S .
. A . D . I . D . M . S .
U N C U R B E D . A C H Y
. N . T . R . L . G . E .
M A R Y B A K E R E D D Y
```

134

```
H U R L E D . B Y L A W S
E . I . V . C . A . R . H
C O N C I S E . C O T T A
T . G . L . M . H . I . N
O Z O N E . E N T I C E D
R . . . Y . N . . . L . Y
. C O M E S T I B L E S .
A . V . M . O . . . . . R
C H E Z M O I . S H A D E
R . R . I . X . W . B . G
O I L E D . E R E L O N G
S . A . G . R . L . U . A
S E P T E T . C L O T H E
```

135

```
Z E R O T O L E R A N C E
I . A . I . U . O . O . X
P A I N F U L . S E T U P
. . L . F . L . I . E . E
B A W L . R E V E R S E D
A . A . G . D . L . . . I
C E Y L O N . G E T O U T
K . . . O . F . E . N . E
W I T H D R A W . H E L D
A . I . W . T . G . R . .
T A B O O . H A R B O U R
E . I . O . O . I . U . U
R O A L D A M U N D S E N
```

136

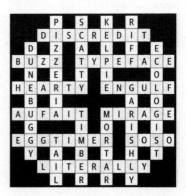

266

137

```
S I N I S T E R   L A I C
E   O   E   L   B R   A
C A M E L   I N R U I N S
T   I   F   J   E   E T
  A N T I M A C A S S A R
B   A   N   H   T     A
L O L I T A   C H A L E T
U     E   P   E   I   O
D E T E R I O R A T E D
G   R   E   N   G   D I
E L A P S E D   A L O U D
O   P   T   E   I   W L
N A S H   O R D N A N C E
```

138

```
C A T C H U N A W A R E S
A   R   A   A   A   A U
D R A I N E R   N A P E S
    I   G   R   D   I P
B A L E   B O N E I D L E
Y   E   O   W   R     N
S H R O U D   B E H E A D
T     T   B   R   L   E
A L L U S I O N   T I E R
N   O   I   V   T   C R
D I C E D   I M A G I N E
E   U   E   N   T   T L
R E M O R S E L E S S L Y
```

139

```
  R E C K O N   C L O U D
  E   R   I   L   V   E
A S S I G N   C A V E R N
  P   N   T   S   R   U
W I N G   M I S H E A R D
  T   E   E K   L   E
  E N D I N G I T A L L
O   I   T   N   P   O
P A R T I S A N   P I T S
T   V   N   Y   L   I
O P A Q U E   D E A C O N
U   N   I   I   U   N
T O A S T   S P A D E S
```

140

```
S U P P L E M E N T A R Y
O   H   O   U   A P   E
B E A C O N S   U R A L S
    L   K   I   S R   T
D R A G   U N S E T T L E
E   N   G   G   O     R
B O X E R S   S U N B E D
A     A   A   S   A   A
T E S T T U B E   P L O Y
A   T   E   O   F   I
B R I E F   D O L P H I N
L   E   U   E   E   A A
E A S Y L I S T E N I N G
```

SOLUTIONS

141

	S	K	Y	M	A	R	S	H	A	L	
A		P		A		N		E		N	
G	O	L	D	W	Y	N		V	E	G	A	N
G		I		L		E		E		L		A
R	O	T	S		E	X	E	R	T	I	O	N
A			A		E		I		I		N	O
V	A	C	A	N	T		S	T	A	G	E	S
A		H		C		A		Y				E
T	R	A	V	E	S	T	Y		E	P	I	C
E		M		S		T		F		R		O
D	E	B	U	T		I	B	E	R	I	A	N
		E		R		L		E		O		D
	G	R	E	Y	M	A	T	T	E	R		

142

A	C	C	E	P	T		A	F	F	O	R	D
U		H		A			A		B		U	
T	R	A	P	S		P	E	N	N	A	N	T
U		N		T		R		F		M		I
M	A	G	N	A	T	E		A	G	A	P	E	S
N		E				S		R				S
	D	A	U	N	T	L	E	S	S		
W		N		A				O		A
R	E	B	U	S		T	A	C	K	L	E	D
I		A		P		Y		E		U		A
G	A	L	L	E	O	N		D	E	B	U	G
H		S		N				E		L		E
T	R	A	C	T	S		A	D	D	E	R	S

143

H	E	A	D	S	W	I	L	L	R	O	L	L
E		U		A		G		E		N		O
L	I	T		F	A	N	T	A	S	T	I	C
O		H		E		O		D		H		A
T	R	E	A	S	U	R	E		F	E	L	T
		N		E		E		P		S		E
F	A	T	C	A	T		R	I	B	A	L	D
U		I		T		D		M		M		
R	I	C	E		F	A	R	E	W	E	L	L
N		A		D		M		N		P		O
I	N	T	R	A	N	S	I	T		A	F	T
S		E		L		O		O		G		U
H	E	D	G	E	O	N	E	S	B	E	T	S

144

D	I	G	S		N	A	T	I	O	N	A	L
O		L		M		N		O		U
G	E	A	R		S	A	L	V	A	D	O	R
S		D		T		Z		A		S		K
B	A	R	C	A	R	O	L	L	E		
O		A		N		N		U		F		U
D	U	G	O	N	G		M	A	T	R	O	N
Y		S		H		S		B		O		D
			C	A	N	T	A	L	O	U	P	E
F		S		U		E		E		F		R
U	N	W	A	S	H	E	D		B	R	A	W
S		A		E		D				O		A
S	U	N	D	R	E	S	S		Q	U	A	Y

145

```
C O S T A R I C A   S   S
  B   W   U   A   H U S H
B E G I N N I N G   R   A
  Y   N   O   D   I R O N
L   A   C U P I D   O   G
I N S U L T   D A G G E R
E   T   O       I   A   I
G H O S T S   B R U T A L
E   U   H A I R Y   E   A
L Y N X   T   A   T   I
O   D   S I G N O R I N A
R E E F   R   C   A   N
D   D   M E T H O D I S T
```

146

```
      T O R M E N T E D
C D U   U   C   I     I
H O I S T   E X H U M E S
E   L   O   F   O   E   E
S O L A R I U M   T H I N
T   Y   I   L   G   O   C
E N D E A R   D R E N C H
R   A   L   B   E   O   A
F I L O   S I D E B U R N
I   L   F   C   N   R   T
E D I F I C E   T H E M E
L   E   F   P   E   D   D
D Y S P E P S I A
```

147

```
  B I S E C T   F A C E T
  A   L   R   R   O     W
S I L A G E   L O U N G E
I   C   S     Z   S     E
R I S K   C U B E R O O T
F   E   E   A   L     S
  F U N A N D G A M E S
O   G   D   A   E   Q
G L A S N O S T   L A U D
R   N   I   E   A   E
I N D I C T   L I N T E L
S   A   H   L   G   Z
H E N C E   D E L E T E
```

148

```
M A G N E T I C N O R T H
A   E   S   R   O   E   I
N U T   P R O B O S C I S
I   T   R   N   K   O   T
A T H L E T I C   E R G O
  E   S   C   D   D   R
O P P O S E   B U B B L Y
L   I   O   C   M   R
Y U C K   D O U B L E U P
M   T   S   G   B   A   O
P R U R I E N C E   K I T
U   R   F   A   L   E   T
S P E C T A C U L A R L Y
```

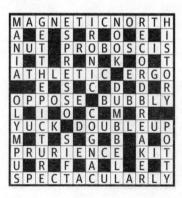

SOLUTIONS

149

```
A P P E N D   G E E U P
N   E     E   R   M   A
F A R R O W   D A P P E R
G   I     S   P   E   A
C R U D   A N C H O R E D
A   O     G   U   O   E
M O T H E R B O A R D
W   C     N   B   R   O
A R T I S T R Y   T H U D
L   O     I   H   I   B
N A P A L M   O C C U L T
U   U     K   L   L   E
T A S T Y   D E F E A T
```

150

```
B R I G H T   A C E T I C
O   N   E     A   R   O
W A F E R   F O R T I F Y
M   I   O   R   I   C   O
A N D A N T E   B L E A T
N   E   E     O   E
  L O U D M O U T H
L   T   A     E   G
E R A T O   S A L S I F Y
T   S   P   O   A   R   P
F U S T I A N   S P E C S
L   A   A     S   S   U
Y E M E N I   P O S S U M
```

151

```
N O F E A R   A S H R A M
A   R   S E   H   E   I
T R A N S O M   O R G A N
I   U   U B   P   A   N
V O D K A   R I S O T T O
E   G   O     T   W
  U N D E R C A N V A S
S   E   A     O   C
H A T C H E T   M A R S H
A   T E   I   I   O   A
M E L O N   O M N I B U S
E   E C   N   E   O   E
D O D G E R   H E A T E D
```

152

```
  A S D R Y A S D U S T
B   I   E   N   O O   C
I N T U R M O I L   M A R A
T     E   R   C   M     A
E L A N D   A G E L E S S
T   R   O   K     L     H
H A R A S S   F I N I S H
E   O     B   N   E   E
D O G S T A R   C O R A L
U   A   R   O   H     M
S O N   E X O N E R A T E
T   C   A   C   C   W   T
  B E N T T H E K N E E
```

153

```
C I R C U M F E R E N C E
O   E   S   R   U   O   X
S A N R E M O   S C R A P
    A   S   L   S   T   E
L O U D   F I N I S H E D
H   L   G   C   A       I
A U T H O R   I N N A T E
S   L   A   S   S       N
A C C I D E N T   L O F T
A   R   L   G   G   F
P E E V E   O B L O N G S
S   S   A   R   U   O   L
O U T O F H A R M S W A Y
```

154

```
    F   C   H   B
B E L E A G U E R E D
E   A   S   N   U   E
T R E K   S U C C I N C T
E       O   H   S   O
C A P R I C E   F E R R Y
V   E   K   G   R   A
W E L L S   P U L S A T E
M   I   K   M       I
D E N A R I U S   P R O W
N   B   O   H   R   N
T E L L S T O R I E S
    E   K   E   M
```

155

```
I N B L O O M   D   S   G
M   O   N   A L I B A B A
B E R S E R K   S   F   M
D I N G O   E X C L A I M
  D   R   I   O   R   O
  E   R E T E N T I O N
    E   T   C       A
S A F E H O U S E   T
H   U   E   N   R I G H T
A D M I R E R   T   O   W
B   I   O   E P I C U R E
B A N D A N A   N   D   E
Y   G   D   L A G G A R D
```

156

```
  P A L M S P R I N G S
P   X   E   U   B   U   S
O V E R T U R E S   E C U
S   H   I   E   S   P
S A M B A   F I N E S S E
I   A   N   Y   W   R
B U S K E R   C O H O R T
I   S   H   L   R   A
L U M B A G O   Y U K O N
I   E   I   A   M   K
T E D   S A X O P H O N E
Y   I   L   E   I   A   R
  M A D E I R A C A K E
```

SOLUTIONS

157

158

159

160

161

```
M I X E D M E T A P H O R
 M   X     I   H   R   V
S P I T   S A R D O N I C
 U   R   S   O   V     D
I N S A T I A B L E   R
 I     L       R   B
S T O O G E   B U B B L Y
 Y   P     A       U
     E A S Y S T R E E T
 V   N   A   M   I   M
B A S I L I C A   V I O L
 S   N   N   T   E   O
W E I G H T L I F T I N G
```

162

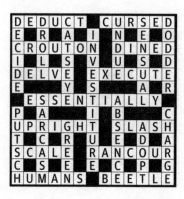

```
D E D U C T   C U R S E D
E   R   A   I   N   E   O
C R O U T O N   D I N E D
I   L   S   V   U   S   D
D E L V E   E X E C U T E R
E       Y   S       A   R
  E S S E N T I A L L Y
P   A     I   B       C
U P R I G H T   S L A S H
T   C   R   U   E   D   A
S C A L E   R A N C O U R G
C   S   E   E   C   P   G
H U M A N S   B E E T L E
```

163

```
D I R E   E C L I P S E D
E   I   G   H   N   E   O
A D V E R S E   P A N E L
D   E   A   R   U   D   E
L E T U P   R A T I O N
O       P   Y       F   S
C A T H A Y P A C I F I C
K   A     I   O       O
  C L I N I C   G O F A R
S   L   O   K   N   L   N
W A I S T   I N A H U F F
I   N   C   N   C   K   U
M A N C H E G O   B E L L
```

164

```
  P A R L O U R G A M E
N   S   I   N   O   Y   S
I M P L A N T E D   T A T
G   I   I   L   H   A
H U M U S   D A Y B O O K
T   A   E   Y   L   K
I N R U S H   S M O O C H
N   C   M   O   G   O
G E O R G I A   R O Y A L
A   P   A   N   E   D
L E O   B A T T L E A X E
E   L   L   I   L   P   R
  B O X E R S H O R T S
```

SOLUTIONS

165

A	L	L	B	E	T	S	A	R	E	O	F	F
	U		E		R		G		M		A	
I	S	I	S		A	T	A	P	I	N	C	H
	C		E		N		I		N		E	
S	I	X	T	H	S	E	N	S	E		H	
	O			I				N			H	
P	U	N	D	I	T		E	X	T	R	A	S
	S		I			V				R		
		C	L	A	V	I	C	H	O	R	D	
	M		K		M		L		E		I	
R	E	S	E	M	B	L	E		A	I	D	E
	T		N		E		Y		R		A	
T	H	E	S	E	R	P	E	N	T	I	N	E

166

| | | | | | | | | | | | | | |
|C|U|S|P| |T|H|O|R|A|C|I|C|
|O| |K| |S| |U| |A| |O| |R|
|Q|U|I|T|T|E|R| |T|A|N|G|A|
|A| |R| |A| |R| |E| |S| |B|
U	T	T	E	R		I	N	D	E	E	D	
V			E		C				N			A
I	N	T	E	R	G	A	L	A	C	T	I	C
N		H			N		R					A
	M	U	M	B	L	E		M	U	G	U	P
M		S	A		L		L		L	A		U
E	L	F	I	N		A	S	E	X	U	A	L
S		A		T		M		T		D		C
H	A	R	R	U	M	P	H		T	Y	P	O

167

			Z		S		W		B			
	J	O	I	N	T	H	E	C	L	U	B	
	U		N		U		L		A		A	
S	M	U	G		F	I	S	H	C	A	K	E
	P			F		H		K		E		
H	I	P	S	T	E	R		S	O	R	R	Y
	N		H		D		D		U		S	
A	G	L	O	W		C	U	S	T	O	D	Y
	B		R		B		S				O	
S	E	A	T	R	O	U	T		F	I	Z	Z
	A		A		O		B		L		E	
	N	I	G	H	T	V	I	S	I	O	N	
			E		H		N		T			

168

| | | | | | | | | | | | | | |
|S|U|M|O|W|R|E|S|T|L|I|N|G|
|O| |A| |I| |L| |E| |N| |E|
|F|O|R| |P|R|E|S|E|A|S|O|N|
|I| |Q| |E| |V| |N| |E| |O|
A	M	U	N	D	S	E	N		A	C	H	E
		I		O		N		S		T		S
H	U	S	H	U	P		S	T	R	I	K	E
U		D		T		C		R		V		
M	I	E	N		C	A	K	E	H	O	L	E
E		S		S		N		N		R		I
R	E	A	S	O	N	I	N	G		O	D	D
U		D		U		N		T		U		E
S	T	E	E	P	L	E	C	H	A	S	E	R

169

170

171

172

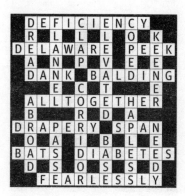

SOLUTIONS

173

174

175

176

177

178

179

180

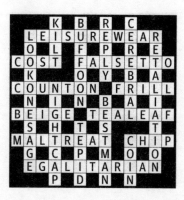

SOLUTIONS

181

S	T	A	T	E	S	M	A	N	S	H	I	P
T		U		N		E		O		E		R
O	P	T		C	O	M	E	O	F	A	G	E
O		H		R		B		N		T		C
L	O	O	K	O	V	E	R		S	H	O	E
		R		A		R		F		R		P
C	L	I	N	C	H		C	A	V	O	R	T
O		T		H		F		S		B		
N	O	A	H		C	U	R	T	A	I	N	S
T		R		H		T		E		N		I
A	G	I	T	A	T	I	O	N		S	U	N
I		A		F		L		E		O		C
N	O	N	A	T	T	E	N	D	A	N	C	E

182

183

184

| L | A | M | P | O | O | N | E | D |

185

186

```
  A S O F T E N A S N O T
S   P A R   M A   U
T R O U T   M O B S T E R
A   R   E   I   I A   N
G I R L   A N A T O L I A
E   A   E   E   I     D
M U N I C H   T O N G U E
A     S   A   N   O   A
N U G A T O R Y   B U F F
A   A   A G   A   A   E
G A V O T T E   L Y C R A R
E   E   I N   A   H   R
D E L I C A T E S S E N
```

187

188

```
      S   P   S   F
  S U P E R F L U I T Y
  Y   A   E   U N   E
E N V Y   C A S U A L L Y
C     I   H   N   L
C H E M I S E   S C O O P
R   O   E   N   E   W
B O N U S   G O D D E S S
N   R   L   I       T
R O U N D E R S   B O O K
U   F   A   O   E   N
S Q U A R E M E T R E
    L   N   E   S
```

SOLUTIONS

189

```
D E B T O R · B R A C E R
I · A · F · C · E · H · A
D O N E F O R · B A I L S
D · J · P · E · U · C · H
L O O S E · A C T U A T E
E · A · M · · · N · · · R
· S M O K E S C R E E N ·
B · I · H · O · · · · · D
E S S E N C E · S T A I R
A · S · U · R · S · R · E
T R I E R · R U I N O U S
E · O · S · Y · N · S · S
R E N D E R · N I C E L Y
```

190

```
P O R R I D G E · · D A U B
O · U · D · R · I · P · E
S I N A I · U N N E R V E
H · A · O · B · A · I · T
· S W A S H B U C K L E R
B · A · Y · Y · C · · · O
A N Y O N E · P E D A L O
B · · · C · T · S · V · T
U N D E R D R E S S E D ·
S · U · A · O · I · R · O
H A C K S A W · B R A S H
K · A · Y · E · L · G · M
A R T Y · C L U E L E S S
```

191

```
E L A P S E · B A R R E D
X · D · T · P · S · U · R
C O M P E R E · H E F T Y
I · I · A · R · E · F · D
T O T A L · S U N R I S E
E · · · T · O · A · N · ·
· E N C H A N T M E N T ·
P · I · · · A · A · · · P
L I B E R A L · D O U S E
U · B · I · O · N · · · P
R U L E D · T A N K T O P
A · E · E · Y · N · I · E
L U S T R E · P A L L O R
```

192

```
· · S · S · P · M · · · ·
· D I S T U R B E D · ·
S · D · A · A · E · B
C I T E · M I N S T R E L
T · S · E · K · · · L
S U M M O N · S H I E L D
A · A · · · · · N · I
A T O N C E · I N F E C T
I · · · Q · N · A · O
G O O D G U Y S · M A S T
N · A · I · I · O · E
· G R O T E S Q U E ·
· · T · Y · T · S · ·
```

193

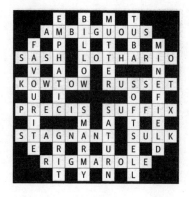

194

195

196

SOLUTIONS

197

	C	A	U	S	E	C	E	L	E	B	R	E
D		S		H		U		A		R		L
A	P	P	L	E		R	O	M	A	I	N	E
R		H		D		L		P		D		C
B	L	A	G		T	E	N	E	M	E	N	T
Y		L		O		W		T				R
A	C	T	I	N	G		M	E	R	I	N	O
N			E		U		R		D		L	
D	E	A	D	L	I	N	E		L	I	L	Y
J		L		I		B		F		O		S
O	R	L	A	N	D	O		L	A	T	H	I
A		O		E		R		A		I		S
N	E	W	B	R	U	N	S	W	I	C	K	

198

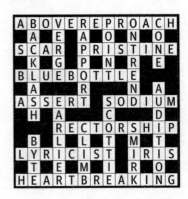

A	B	O	V	E	R	E	P	R	O	A	C	H
	A		E		A		O		N		O	
S	C	A	R		P	R	I	S	T	I	N	E
	K		G		P		N		R		E	
B	L	U	E	B	O	T	T	L	E			
	A		R		R		N		N		A	
A	S	S	E	R	T		S	O	D	I	U	M
	H		A		C				D		M	
		R	E	C	T	O	R	S	H	I	P	
	B		L		T		M		T		T	
L	Y	R	I	C	I	S	T		I	R	I	S
	T		E		M		I		R		O	
H	E	A	R	T	B	R	E	A	K	I	N	G

199

			W	I	S	C	O	N	S	I	N	
J		L		A		I		T		U		O
O	D	O	U	R		S	E	T	U	P	O	N
H		N		D		T		O		E		C
A	S	S	O	R	T	E	D		A	R	C	H
N		D		O		R		L		C		A
N	E	A	R	B	Y		D	E	N	I	A	L
E		L		E		T		G		L		A
S	E	E	K		Q	U	E	S	T	I	O	N
B		B		G		S		T		O		T
U	S	E	L	E	S	S		U	S	U	A	L
R		L		M		L		M		S		Y
G	O	T	O	S	L	E	E	P				

200

D	E	A	D	A	N	D	B	U	R	I	E	D
	V		A		O		E		E		D	
B	E	A	N		M	I	N	I	S	T	E	R
	N		C		A		I		P		N	
A	T	T	E	N	D	A	N	C	E			
	F				I				C		P	
Q	U	E	B	E	C		C	A	T	E	R	S
	L		A				O				E	
		D	I	S	C	U	R	S	I	V	E	
D		F		C		N		H		I		
R	I	G	O	R	O	U	S		R	O	O	K
N		R		U		E		U		U		
D	E	R	M	A	T	O	L	O	G	I	S	T

201

```
W A T E R S O F T E N E R
  Q   G   A   L   S   U
B U N G   W R A P P E R S
  A   O   D   K   O   O
A R T N O U V E A U   S
  I       S       S   C
G U L L E T   G A E L I C
  M   I       A       N
    B E F O R E H A N D
  X   E   A   B   U   A
U M B R E L L A   N U M B
  A   I   S   G   C   O
A S I A N E L E P H A N T
```

202

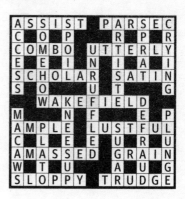

```
A S S I S T   P A R S E C
C   O   P     R   P   R
C O M B O   U T T E R L Y
E   E   I   N   I   A   I
S C H O L A R   S A T I N G
S       O     U   T   G
    W A K E F I E L D
M     N   F     E   P
A M P L E   L U S T F U L
C   L   E   E   U   R   U
A M A S S E D   G R A I N
W   T   U     A   U   G
S L O P P Y   T R U D G E
```

203

```
L O B E   P H Y S I C A L
E   E   B   E   E   O   U
F U N F A I R   R O L E S
T   I   N   O   U   O   T
W O N G A   I M M U N E
I   N   C       E   W
N U I S A N C E V A L U E
G   C   O   A   R
  V I S H N U   L A P S E
S   N   I   P   I   A   W
C R E E K   L E S O T H O
U   S   E   E   E   C   L
D I S C R E T E   C H E F
```

204

```
  C H E S T E R F I E L D
G   E   A   N   L   T   E
I N L E T   C H E K H O V
A   I   E   O   E   I   I
N I C E   P R O T O C O L
T   A   L   E   I     M
K E L V I N   E N I G M A
I     T   K   G   R   Y
L I S T E R I A   T A L C
L   N   R   T   B   P   A
I S O B A R S   A B H O R
N   U   T   C   K   I   E
G E T R I C H Q U I C K
```

SOLUTIONS

205

206

207

208

209

```
W I N G C O M M A N D E R
I   E   O   O   W   E   O
L A X   L A S P A L M A S
D   T   O   T   Y   O   E
E N T I R E L Y   K N I T
    O   A   Y   S   S   T
C A N A D A   B I S T R E
L   O   O   S   D   R
A L T O   F O R E C A S T
N   H   G   L   R   T   A
G O I T A L O N E   I L L
E   N   L   N   A   V   L
R O G U E S G A L L E R Y
```

210

```
  B L O U S E   B A B E L
  U   C   I   L   I   U
S T R A N D   M A T R I X
  T   R   E   Z   E   U
G O B I   S E M E S T E R
  N   N   W   I   T   Y
  S H A V I N G F O A M
G   A   P   R   S   O
I N C A M E R A   T W I N
B   K   A   T   R   S
B A N D I T   O P I A T E
E   E   Z   R   C   E
T H Y M E   H Y P H E N
```

211

```
B I R D S N E S T S O U P
U   A   O   Q   I   U   O
M A C   C O U P D E T A T
P   K   A   I   Y   B   T
Y E A R L I N G   G O R E
    N   L   E   D   A   R
G A D G E T   N E A R B Y
I   P   D   H   J   D
M A I D   L I N E S M A N
M   N   P   J   C   O   I
I T I N E R A N T   T O M
C   O   R   C   E   O   B
K E N T U C K Y D E R B Y
```

212

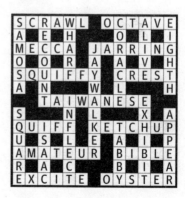

```
S C R A W L   O C T A V E
A   E   H   O   L   I
M E C C A   J A R R I N G
O   O   R   A   A   V   H
S Q U I F F Y   C R E S T
A   N   W   L   H
  T A I W A N E S E
S   N   L   X   A
Q U I F F   K E T C H U P
U   S   L   E   A   I   P
A M A T E U R   B I B L E
R   A   C   B   I   A
E X C I T E   O Y S T E R
```

SOLUTIONS

213

214

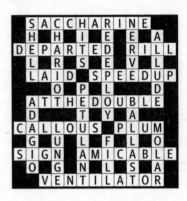

215

216

217

```
B A D I N A G E _ A B E D
U _ E _ O _ U _ F _ L _ O
G I V E N _ F A R M I N G
S _ I _ E _ F _ O _ S _ G
_ M O N T P A R N A S S E
A _ U _ H _ W _ T _ _ R _
C A S H E W _ C I R C L E
O _ W _ S _ S _ H _ _ L _
U N P R I N C I P L E D _
S _ E _ S _ O _ I _ N _ W
T O R R E N T _ E N N U I
I _ K _ R _ C _ C _ A _ S
C A S K _ S H E E P I S H
```

218

```
O N L Y _ S C A F F O L D
V _ U _ C _ O _ I _ F _ U
E X C L A I M _ G A F F E
R _ R _ S _ P _ H _ E _ L
S L E E T _ R A T I N G _
E _ _ L _ E _ _ _ C _ A _
A T T H E S H A R P E N D
S _ A _ _ E _ U _ _ _ H _
_ C R A V E N _ B L A Z E
Y _ N _ E _ S _ A _ B _ R
A L I E N _ I N T R U D E
K _ S _ O _ O _ O _ S _ N
S C H E M I N G _ P E S T
```

219

```
C O S H _ B O T H E R E D
R _ M _ V _ U _ O _ _ O _
E G A D _ D E T R I T U S
O _ S _ H _ R _ D _ H _ H
S C H O O L D A Y S _ _ _
O _ H _ B _ O _ G _ J _ S
T R I L B Y _ A U G U S T
E _ T _ Y _ E _ R _ B _ E
_ _ W H I S T D R I V E _
O _ S _ O _ T _ Y _ L _ P
P A P E R B A G _ M A L I
E _ O _ S _ T _ _ N _ S _
N A T T E R E D _ E T C H
```

220

```
_ D O L L A R S I G N _ _
O _ A _ I _ I _ R _ F _ _
B R I C K R E D _ A P E X
I _ Q _ Y _ E _ N _ L _ _
C R U X _ S K I D R O W _
E _ _ F _ I _ _ _ _ N _ _
P E R F U N C T O R Y _ _
E _ _ L _ K _ N _ _ _ _ _
F L Y H A L F _ B L U B _
V _ I _ B _ S _ E _ A _ _
L I O N _ E Y E P A T C H
S _ D _ A _ E _ V _ O _ _
_ C U R M U D G E O N _ _
```

SOLUTIONS

221

```
  F U N D A M E N T A L
B   L   I   I   I   D   F
L E T H A R G I C   J A R
A   A   L   H   E   O   A
C R I M E   T O R S I O N
K   R   C   Y   N   N   K
B E A U T Y   R E L I E F
O   S   C   A   N   U
T O C C A T A   R O G E R
T   I   L   S   L   S   R
O R B   I N T R I C A T E
M   L   A   R   E   S   R
  S E I S M O G R A P H
```

222

```
F A R M H A N D S   P   M
  X   O   P   I   M E N U
M I N T S A U C E   T   L
  S   H   T   T   G R I T
S   C   G H O U L   O   I
H O O K E Y   M E R L O T
A   M   T   V   E   U
D U M D U M   G E R U N D
O   O   P U P I L   M   E
W I N E   T   F   S   T
B   L   S A N T A C R U Z
O V A L   T   E   A   B
X   W   T E D D Y B E A R
```

223

```
  D E V I C E   C H A R R
W   I   O   R   Q   U
L E S S O N   D E L U X E
  L   I   S   T   E   I
C L O T   C A R E W O R N
O   O   I   I   U   G
  N E R V O U S N E S S
S   D   U   K   N   E
T H I C K S E T   T A R N
O   F   R   A   E   V
C R I T I C   K A N S A S
K   C   L   E   T   N
S T E A L   U R G E N T
```

224

```
    T R A F F I C J A M
P   I   R   i   H   W
R E D C A R D   A S K E W
I   E   K   D   R   W   E
Z E S T   B L A C K A R T
E       C   Y   O   R   B
F I C K L E   S A N D A L
I   H   U   H   L       A
G O O S E G O G   S P I N
H   R   L   W   S   R   K
T R I P E   Z I P C O D E
  Z   S   A   A   X   T
T O P S Y T U R V Y
```